ICE CREAM IS EXQUISITE. WHAT A PITY IT IS NOT ILLEGAL. VOLTAIRE

First published in Great Britain in 2012
by Mitchell Beazley, an imprint of
Octopus Publishing Group Limited, Endeavour House,
189 Shaftesbury Avenue, London, WC2H 8JY

An Hachette UK Company
www.hachette.co.uk

This edition published 2013
Distributed in the US by Hachette Book Group USA,
237 Park Avenue, New York, NY 10017, USA
www.octopusbooksusa.com

Distributed in Canada by Canadian Manda Group,
165 Dufferin Street, Toronto, Ontario, Canada M6K 3H6

978-1-84533-762-9
Set in Quadraat, Trajan, Monster Days and Drunken Shower. Printed and bound in China.

Commissioning Editor: Eleanor Maxfield | Art Direction & Design: Yasia Williams-Leedham
Photography: Anders Schonnemann | Home Economist: Laura Fyfe
Props Styling: Rachel Jukes | Production: Caroline Alberti
Editor: Jo Wilson | Copy Editor: Patricia Burgess
Proofreader: Kate Fox | Indexer: Hilary Bird

Note: Some recipes contain nuts and nut derivatives. Anyone with a known
nut allergy must avoid these. This book contains some dishes made with
raw or lightly cooked eggs. It is prudent for more vulnerable people such as
pregnant and nursing mothers, people with weakened immune systems, the elderly,
babies, and young children, to avoid raw or lightly cooked eggs.

Contents

INTRODUCTION: THE SCOOP, THE WHOLE SCOOP, AND NOTHING BUT THE SCOOP

There is nothing more incongruous than the collision of unforeseen and spectacular life-changing events that led to the creation of The Icecreamists. It began when I was an excitable, stuttering, five-year-old seaside boy, waiting for my father to buy me my first-ever ice cream cone as I gripped a stick of candy in one hand and a souvenir hat in the other.

We lived on what we affectionately called "Planet Thanet," a piece of chalky rock bobbing around at the southern end of the North Sea, surrounded by the crumbling English seaside towns of Margate, Ramsgate, and Broadstairs. As I left the ice cream parlor on Margate seafront, I used a chocolate candy bar to press the ice cream gently down into the cone to make sure every mouthful consisted of softly whipped ice cream and crunchy cone pieces.

But I was then to experience for the first time the bittersweet pain of loss, when juggling my stick of candy and hat, I dropped my frozen treat onto the seafront. My father couldn't help but laugh as I stood weeping, ice cream dripping down my T-shirt and melting into the pores of the concrete promenade. The sadness and humor in what that dropped ice cream represented remains with me to this day: a reminder that, like childhood, life passes all too soon; innocence lost, melting away in a decaying seaside town.

From that early age, my fascination with ice cream was not only enduring, but became a metaphor for life: it was fickle, fleeting, fragile, and in a permanent state of flux. It is no exaggeration to say it would shape my life emotionally, physically, and politically.

After I escaped from Planet Thanet, there followed a 20-year career in ice cream as a consultant for the likes of Unilever and Mars, before becoming creative director on major ice cream brands and launching the UK's first Italian gelato, "Antonio Federici."

Even when I faced profound personal challenges after losing contact with my children during a divorce, I found solace and inspiration in ice cream.

NOTHING ELSE ON GOD'S EARTH CONNECTED ME TO MY INNER CHILD LIKE THE MEMORY OF MY FIRST ICE CREAM CONE

I was the same excitable 5-year-old boy from Planet Thanet, but trapped in the body of a 40-year-old man.

ICECREAMIST: A PERSON ADDICTED TO OR OBSESSED WITH ICE CREAM. *"AN EXTREME ICE CREAM FANATIC."* ICECREAMISM CAN BE HIGHLY ADDICTIVE AND INFECTIOUS.

In 2008, I persuaded my family to join me on my deranged adventure with some research trips, first to New York, and then to the beguiling, jewel-encrusted coves of the Italian riviera and the shimmering ports of Portofino and Rapallo. From there, I studied with Italian gelato master Roberto Lobrano and realized that while Italian gelato was the Holy Grail for an ice cream evangelist like me, it was bound by a frustratingly rigid set of Italian traditions and codes. As I pursued the idea of an experimental ice cream concept, I found a whole plethora of facts that would seed the idea in my head, of ice cream as a medium for political protest.

To my mind, it could be elevated to another level by cold-fusing it with cocktail techniques and pop culture influences to create ice cream from another dimension. Of course, this was heresy to many of my Italian colleagues, but Roberto rose to the challenge, producing sublime gelatos that transported artisan ice cream to vertiginous new heights.

I then tapped into my melting pot of other influences, cross-fertilizing ideas from abstract reference points with a team of chefs and cocktail mixologists. We put ice cream on toast, added popping candy that would blow your fillings out, we blowtorched ice cream at the table, flamed another with a shot of 90 percent homemade chili vodka—all in an attempt to satiate my pyromaniac tendencies.

The final chapter in the development of the whipped-up, mixed-up, upside-down world of The Icecreamists was shaped in the various custody suites and police cells I visited during my campaigning days. As the founder of Fathers 4 Justice, I had a background in staging dramatic, high-profile events that explored the outer extremities of the law and breached national security with alarming frequency—much to the chagrin of the British government.

This coincided with a fashionably brief stint in rehab, where I concluded that ice cream had previously unrealized addictive and hallucinatory properties. The idea of "icecreamism" was born in a *One Flew Over the Cuckoo's Nest* moment as I challenged patients to "lick their addiction" with Randle P. McMurphy gusto. "Take me to my dealer!" I would announce to the nursing staff as I berated my Librium-popping pals for their overenthusiastic consumption of drugs designed to knock them into a catatonic stupor.

I CONCLUDED THERE AND THEN, THERE COULD BE NO BETTER MEDIUM THAN ICE CREAM TO CELEBRATE THE CULTURE OF ADDICTION

In June 2008, I had retired from frontline campaigning to devote the next few years of my life to this as yet unnamed ice cream project. Scotland Yard, concerned that my move into ice cream might be some elaborate cover story for the overthrow of the British government (I kid not), sent two officers from Counter Terrorism Command down to Romsey in Hampshire, where I was living at the time. As I was being questioned inquisitorially about the authenticity of my love of ice cream, they told me of their concern about "domestic extremists." I fixed my icy gaze on the senior officer and flippantly declared, "I am not an extremist, I am an icecreamist." And there, in that moment of absurdity, sitting in front of counter terrorism police officers, The Icecreamists were born.

My next mission would be to liberate the world, one lick at a time

BRAIN FREEZE

THE HISTORY OF ICE CREAM IS PLAGUED with inaccurate and often fabricated claims. Early evidence of ice cream comes from China between 618 and 907, during the Tang period. King Shang used to have a frozen dish made for him out of buffalo milk, flour, and camphor.

GELATO is credited to Bernardo Buontalenti, a sixteenth-century Florentine, who presented his creation to the court of Catherina de Medici. However, this is disputed; variations of gelato are thought to have existed in similar forms for thousands of years.

THE WORLD'S TOP FIVE consumers of ice cream per capita are the United States, New Zealand, Denmark, Australia, and Belgium.

THE COLDER IT GETS the more ice cream you eat. The highest consumption of ice cream per capita in Europe is in chilly Scandinavia.

ICE CREAM SUNDAES were created when in the late nineteenth century when it was illegal to sell ice cream with flavored soda on a Sunday in the American town of Evanston. Traders circumnavigated the law by serving ice cream with a syrup and calling it an "Ice Cream Sunday." They later replaced the "y" with an "e" to avoid upsetting religious leaders.

CAN YOU LICK IT? Yes you can! American presidents have a long association with ice cream. As a boy, President "Ike" Eisenhower worked as a boy in the ice cream factory of the Belle Springs Creamery Company in Abilene, Kansas. During the 1960 presidential election, voters could choose between the Nixon Bar and the Kennedy Bar, both of which carried pictures of the candidates. President Barack Obama used to work for Baskin Robbins, one of the country's more popular ice cream brands.

RIVAL GANGS in Glasgow, Scotland, used ice cream vans in the 1980s as a cover for selling drugs and stolen goods, resulting in the infamous "Glasgow Ice Cream Wars." Police there were later nicknamed the "Serious Chimes Squad" for their alleged incompetence in dealing with the gang warfare.

IN THE FORMER SOVIET REPUBLIC OF BELARUS "Organized ice cream eating" was banned by the president because it was considered an unauthorized public assembly. Government agents broke up the event, arresting many of the people the government regarded as "extremists." The idea of organized ice cream eating as political protest was born.

BAGHDAD enjoyed more ice cream per capita during the Iraq War than the Americans did in some U.S. cities.

IN THE 2008 GAZA WAR, the Israelis bombed the Al Ameer ice cream factory in Gaza. Owner Yaser Alwadeya said, "I can't figure out why the Israelis thought that Hamas had anything to do with ice cream."

DURING PROHIBITION, major breweries, including Anheuser-Busch and Stroh's, produced barrels of ice cream instead of liquor.

ADOLF HITLER decreed in July 1933 that German ice cream had to contain at least 10 percent milk-fat.

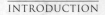
One small lick for man. One giant scoop for mankind

In 2009, as the world was in economic meltdown, The Icecreamists were about to occupy 3,500 square feet of Selfridges department store in London with a subterranean God Save the Cream guerrilla-punk pop-up boutique. This was no ordinary ice cream parlor, but instead a deliciously twisted satanic temple of cool filtered through my febrile imagination. Selfridges rocked to our house band (called, naturally, The Icecreamists), there was a movie theater and we also had an ice cream van covered in political slogans and driven by a dummy of Her Majesty the Queen.

The boutique also dispensed our first infamous ice cream cocktail, The Sex Pistol. This frisky little minx consisted of "natural stimulant" ice cream and a shot of absinthe served from an intravenous drip by Nurse Selena. Not only did this medication need administering, but when we put it in a cone, a newspaper dubbed it the "Whorenetto" (a pun on a British ice cream brand) This was an ice cream with enough erectile properties to raise people from the dead.

But the stimulant ice cream also aroused vast amounts of press attention and controversy. Within days it was "Sex Pistols at dawn," as the punk band I had mistakenly assumed to be dead turned out to be alive and claiming that our ice cream infringed their intellectual copyright of the Queen. I pointed out that our use of the Queen was subverting their subversion of the Queen's image, which they didn't have permission to use in the first place.

We arrived in London's Covent Garden in February 2011 with the snarling, schizophrenic mixture of apocalyptic cool that was our first permanent store. We opened with a "Lick Your Addiction" treatment program of subzero elixirs that had been specifically tailored to treat lapsed hell-raisers, recovering hedonists and practicing satirists, fugitives and diabetics. It was then that my long-suffering benefactor and business partner, the incomparable Frank Frederick, challenged me to create an ice cream story in the middle of winter that would end up on CNN.

I dutifully consulted my vault of recipes and concepts and resurrected the idea of breast milk ice cream.

SOME PEOPLE ARGUED AGAINST THE IDEA, SAYING THAT BREAST MILK WAS A BODILY FLUID, BUT "SO IS COW'S MILK," I REPLIED. "BREAST MILK IS FOR KIDS," SAID OTHERS. "WELL, GUESS WHAT?" I RESPONDED. "COW'S MILK IS FOR CALVES."

WHATEVER IS FUNNY IS SUBVERSIVE. EVERY JOKE IS A CUSTARD PIE. A DIRTY JOKE A SORT OF MENTAL REBELLION. GEORGE ORWELL

Human beings, I had discovered, are the only mammals that drink the milk of other mammals. I was fascinated by society's revulsion to breast milk. This was an opportunity for a taboo-breaking, iconoclastic ice cream.

So it happened. We called it Baby Gaga and advertised for donors on Mumsnet. Fifteen came forward, but I chose mother of one Victoria Hiley. She was an articulate exponent of breast-feeding. She was screened in line with hospital standards and we went ahead and made our first batch. On February 25, 2011, we opened our doors to what became a global phenomenon.

For satirical authenticity, we said the ice cream was freshly squeezed, free roaming, and totally natural, and came served with a shot of teething medicine and a baby teething chew. An added bonus was that it was also suitable for anyone who was lactose intolerant.

We sold out of Baby Gaga ice cream within the first hour. By the second hour, the world's press had descended on our humble emporium. By the evening, we'd been busted by the food fascists from Westminster Council (now dubbed Breastminster Council), who marched in as if they were looking for biohazardous chemical waste, seized two remaining scoops left for the press, and banned Baby Gaga ice cream. As they left, I endeavored to point out that while you could drink and smoke yourself to death in the London Borough of Westminster, there had never been a single recorded death in the history of humanity from the consumption of human breast milk. The fact that breast milk had weaned the world seemed to have escaped them. We responded by placing posters in the window: "Frozen out by Nanny State."

The following Monday the media storm continued and I attracted attention from an outraged pop-megastar Lady Gaga. She declared that Baby Gaga was an infringement of her name and that the ice cream was both "provocative and nausea-inducing."

We now had over 300 breast-milk donors and could have opened a milking parlor instead of an ice cream parlor. Westminster Council admitted they had "boobed" and gave Baby Gaga a clean bill of health, and Lady Gaga eventually realized that the more she threatened us, the more publicity we got.

After repelling the threat of both closure and bankruptcy, we opened our second store in the Piazza, Covent Garden, about a month later. After 40 years, the story of The Icecreamists was complete.

Today, The Icecreamists are shaping a new world of oral gratification with a decadent kaleidoscope of mind-altering icescapades in cold-fused refreshments. We remain a theatrically minded troupe of provocateurs and cold warriors, hopelessly foul-mouthed, anti-Establishment, and politically incorrect. However, we have purged ourselves of our old law-breaking ways and dedicated our lives to converting a cold, cruel, unforgiving world to the life-enhancing gospel of freshly made artisan gelato.

WE SAY ICECREAMISM IS A BIT LIKE CAPITALISM OR SOCIALISM, ONLY FUNNIER, MORE ADDICTIVE, AND BETTER TASTING

You can enjoy it against a bar, against the wall, or against the law.

This is the inside scoop on The Icecreamists. Join me on my mission to boldly go where no ice cream brand has gone before. To liberate the world one lick at a time.

FORGIVE ME, FATHER, FOR I HAVE SINNED

THIS ISN'T YOUR NORMAL RECIPE BOOK—THIS IS PART ICE CREAM BIBLE, PART CONFESSIONAL

Over the years, many people have asked me why they should make their own ice creams and sorbettos when they can easily buy "luxury" ice cream or sorbet from any corner store or supermarket. As an ice cream evangelist, I am naturally biased, but there are a few simple reasons.

First, most so-called luxury ice cream is very high in fat and sugar, and uses a variety of stabilizers and emulsifiers for a long shelf life. The fat masks the flavor of the ice cream, and the other inclusions often cover up the fact that the ice cream itself isn't actually very good. Likewise, store-bought sorbets are often more colorings and concentrates than real fruit. You can make your own delicious organic alternatives at a fraction of the price you pay for it in the store.

Second, nothing can compare to the epiphany you will experience when making fresh ice cream and creating your own flavors. Your relationship with ice cream should be akin to an enduring and dangerous infatuation with a beautiful member of the opposite sex— bewitching, intoxicating, and potentially deadly.

Our boutique ice cream mixes are variations on traditional Italian gelato and are made with a slightly higher fat content for a richer mouthfeel. The strange, subzero alchemy we use to blend whole milk, heavy cream, and egg yolks is the foundation for most of our recipes. Our sorbettos, or water ices, are made from a traditional Italian sugary syrupy base.

SO YOU WANT TO BE AN ICECREAMIST...?

CHOOSE YOUR POISON

You'll find recipes for delicious boutique ice creams and sorbettos for you to master in chapters 1 and 2.

ARM YOURSELF

Decide whether you are making by machine or hand (See pages 14–15).

LOCK AND LOAD

Get tips on tools and ingredients, plus a troubleshooting section (see page 157).

DISCOVER YOUR VICE

Once you've mastered the basic ice creams and sorbettos, you can tackle vice cream cocktails, ice quakes, sundaes, desserts, and ice pops in chapters 3, 4, and 5.

DEVIATE FROM THE SYSTEM

This symbol tells you what delicious variations the featured ice cream or sorbetto is used in. So if you've made A Chocwork Orange ice cream on page 28, you can use it in the Fire and Vice cocktail on page 114.

FIND YOUR MOTHER ICE CREAM

This symbol shows which basic ice cream recipe you'll need to whip up a concoction. So if you like the look of Nuclear Winter ice cream sundae on page 136, you'll need to use Priscilla Cream of the Dessert on page 22.

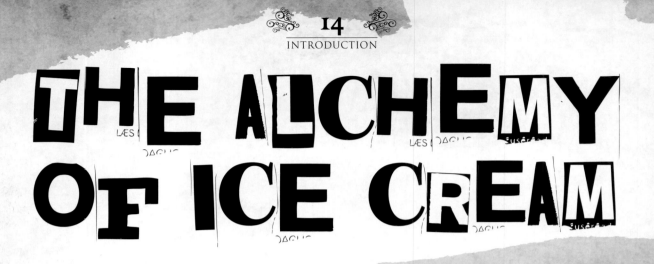

THE ALCHEMY OF ICE CREAM

CHOOSE ME

Choose your recipe and prepare the basic mix at least 12–24 hours ahead of churning the finished ice cream. The mix will take no longer than 20 minutes to put together.

SIZE ME UP

The amount made by each recipe varies slightly, depending on what extra ingredients are added to the base mix.

We recommend making quantities of half the machine's capacity, so 2 cups for a 1-quart machine, because the ice cream expands as the air is churned in, and the machine can struggle if it is filled to the maximum. Also the more mix you put in the machine, the slower the mix will freeze.

The recipes are suitable for a 1-quart machine. If you have a large machine or want to make large batches of ice cream, simply multiply the quantities in the recipes according to the size of the batch you require. Just make sure you've got enough space in your refrigerator for the mix.

TEMPER ME

An ice cream base is composed of heated milk and cream, combined with whisked eggs and sugar. When you pour the hot milk and cream mix onto the egg and sugar mixture, do so gradually and slowly while whisking continuously to temper the eggs and prevent them from scrambling.

The mixture should be heated to no more than 185°F, or until you can see bubbles – about 5 minutes.

CHILL ME

When the mix is ready, pour it into a heatproof bowl and set aside for about 30 minutes, stirring occasionally, until cooled to room temperature. For more rapid chilling, place the bowl in a sink filled halfway with water and some ice for 20 minutes. Don't put the base mixture directly in the refrigerator.

When cooled, cover the mixture and refrigerate, ideally overnight, but at least for 6 hours, until thoroughly chilled to at least 39°F.

WHIP ME

An ice cream machine isn't essential, but we do recommend having one. The results from a good ice cream machine are often so gob-smackingly delicious that they will nearly always surpass your expectations in terms of flavor and mouthfeel.

A machine will make your life easier and the whole process a lot more fun. More importantly, it will pay for itself over and over again. For information on specific types of models, see page 156.

Churning will take about 20–60 minutes, depending on your machine and how cold the mixture is. Always follow the manufacturer's instructions.

BEAT ME

Making ice cream by hand is a traditional and low-cost approach, but it's a lengthy process, and freezing a liquid base mixture into a solid can create nasty hard ice crystals that compromise the smooth and creamy mouthfeel you are trying to achieve. A good immersion blender or electric mixer will make the experience infinitely less demanding. However, if you crave a full cardiac workout to offset diabetes, give beating by hand a whirl.

1. Select a recipe from the book and prepare the mixture according to the recipe.

2. Chill as instructed, then pour the mixture into a plastic container, cover with a lid, and place in your freezer for 50 minutes.

3. Remove from the freezer and beat with an electric mixer or immersion blender to remove ice crystals. Return to the freezer.

4. Over the next 2–3 hours, remove from the freezer every 30 minutes or so and beat again. Finally, keep in the freezer until completely frozen.

SERVE ME

Delivering the perfect serve is a delicate balancing act. Too cold and the ice cream will be difficult to scoop, but too soft and it will melt too quickly. If your ice cream is hard to the touch, let it stand at room temperature for around 5 minutes, or until soft enough to scoop. As with sex, timing is everything!

LICK ME, SUCK ME

When you are making ice cream, it's the flavors that matter, not the color. You should continually taste your mix (using a clean teaspoon) when it is warm and after freezing to be sure you are happy with the flavor. All your ice creams will be a natural, pastel hue. The bright colors you often see in ice cream parlors are achieved by using artificial colorants.

LICK ME QUICK

If you are up against the clock, here is a handy method for making ice cream quickly.

1. Chill the mix as described in step 2 (Beat me).

2. Place the bowl in your freezer on its lowest setting and freeze for 30 minutes, or until the mixture is cold to the touch, stirring occasionally.

3. Pour into an ice cream machine and churn according to the manufacturer's instructions.

4. Once churned pour into a plastic container with a lid and place in the lowest part of your freezer for at least 1½ hours to set.

5. Enjoy!

TEN COMMANDMENTS OF COOL

1. THOU WILL FOLLOW THE COMMANDMENTS

We encourage you to start with our basic boutique ice cream recipes—what we call our Twisted Classics—religiously until you get them just right. After that you can deviate from the recipes (and we always encourage deviation at The Icecreamists). During the flavoring and freezing processes, you will be able to conjure up other flavors with miraculous simplicity and flair.

2. THOU WILL NOT BE INTIMIDATED BY THE GORGEOUS PHOTOGRAPHY

This book is idiot-proof. How do I know? It was road tested on me. Many years ago, when I went to make my first batch of ice cream, I stood looking at my brand new machine and complained to my wife that it looked "absolutely filthy." She shot me a withering look and told me it was our old breadmaker. If I can make a career out of ice cream after that, you can surely make great ice cream.

3. THOU WILL FREEZE YOUR ASSETS

Keep everything—milk, cream, ice cream mixture, fruit, and other ingredients—super-chilled in your refrigerator. This will assist during the production process and help give your ice cream the smooth, luxurious mouthfeel you desire. If you have space, keep your the beaters for your mixers and mixing bowls in the refrigerator, too, or at the very least in the coolest part of your house. You can also chill the plastic container.

4. THOU WILL NEVER COMPROMISE ON INGREDIENTS

The quality of the ingredients you use will have a direct impact on the flavor of your ice cream. Always use seasonal produce whenever possible, especially when choosing fruit for sorbettos. Do not shortchange your ice cream by using artificial sweeteners, low-fat

milks, and suchlike (see page 155). Boutique ice cream already has less fat than standard ice cream, and it needs that fat to create texture and mouthfeel, and to prevent the mixture from developing ice crystals. Moral of the story: if you want to be a choirboy, go to church instead.

5. THOU WILL LEARN THE ART OF PATIENCE

The history of ice cream production is shrouded in historical code, mystery, superstition, and tradition. The real trick is learning the art of patience. You have to make your mixture, then chill it, probably overnight, churn it in an ice cream machine, and freeze it for a few hours—all that even if you are making only as little as a pint. However, it's an ice cream that's been made with a whole lotta love. The joy of making your own is a pleasure you can't measure or put a price on.

6. THOU WILL ENJOY ON THE SAME DAY

The ice creams in this book will keep for up to a week in the freezer, but all homemade ice creams are best enjoyed right away, because the longer they are kept, the icier they will become. Superfresh ice cream is the ultimate indulgence.

7. THOU WILL LET THE ICE CREAM SOFTEN

Every ice maiden should have a soft and scoopable center lying under her permafrost exterior. Always let your ice cream soften for at least 5 minutes at room temperature so it is served at the right consistency. This will also help when scooping.

8. THOU WILL NEVER REFREEZE

Never refreeze or consume ice cream once it has melted. This is what's known in the trade as "temperature abuse." The ice cream will taste gritty, like a mouthful of penguin droppings. You have been warned.

9. THOU WILL LICK YOUR BOWL CLEAN

The ultimate sign of customer satisfaction is when my six-year-old son Archie is holding up the ice cream bowl to his face, drinking the creamy dregs. This might not meet most people's idea of table etiquette, but in the world of The Icecreamists, you have permission to lick your bowl. In fact, we would consider it rude not to.

10. THOU WILL PREPARE YOUR NEXT RECIPE

Now you have accepted your challenge to become an icecreamist, the rules of engagement are as follows: ice cream is not a spectator sport—it's a religion. Get whipping.

QUE *ice creams*

YOUR MISSION, SHOULD YOU CHOOSE TO ACCEPT IT, IS TO CREATE A MIND-ALTERING KALEIDOSCOPE OF VICE CREAMS AND OTHER GUILTY PLEASURES WHILE SAFELY ENSCONCED IN THE BOSOM OF YOUR OWN KITCHEN. FOR PURVEYORS OF ORAL GRATIFICATION, WHAT BETTER PLACE TO START THAN SOME SIMPLE TWISTED CLASSICS? NEXT, MOVE ON TO OUR NOTORIOUS AND LOVABLE ROGUES & ECCENTRICS, AND GET CARRIED AWAY WITH SOME DIET-BUSTING GUILTY PLEASURES, FOLLOWED BY SOME SPIKED CREAMS. FINALLY, WHEN YOUR MISSION IS ACCOMPLISHED AND YOU SUCCUMB TO THE INFECTIOUS SYMPTOMS OF "ICECREAMISM," PLEDGE YOUR ALLEGIANCE WITH THE WORDS "GOD SAVE THE CREAM."

NOTE: ALL THE RECIPES IN THIS CHAPTER TAKE 20 MINUTES TO PREPARE THE BASE MIXTURE OR CUSTARD, 6–24 HOURS FOR CHILLING, AND 20–60 MINUTES FOR CHURNING. ALL RECIPES MAKE ABOUT 2 CUPS (1 PINT), WHICH WILL SERVE FOUR PEOPLE, AND ARE BEST ENJOYED WITHIN A FEW DAYS OF MAKING.

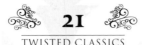

THE VANILLA MONOLOGUES

MADAGASCAN VANILLA ICE CREAM

THIS IS THE MOTHER OF ALL MELTDOWNS—THE ICE CREAM THAT SETS THE BENCHMARK FOR EVERY OTHER IN THIS BOOK. THIS SUBZERO CLASSIC WILL LEAVE YOU MONOLOGUING FOR HOURS. A GREAT VANILLA ICE CREAM MADE WITH SOUL THAT GOES STRAIGHT TO THE HEART.

• **1 cup whole milk** • **½ cup heavy cream** • **1 fat vanilla bean, split lengthwise** • **2 egg yolks** •
⅓ cup plus 1 tablespoon superfine or granulated sugar • **pinch of sea salt**

1. Pour the milk and cream into a large saucepan. Scrape in the vanilla seeds, then add the empty bean and heat gently, stirring occasionally, until the mixture begins to steam but not boil.

2. Meanwhile, whisk the egg yolks in a heatproof bowl until smooth. Add the sugar and salt and whisk until pale and slightly fluffy. Gradually and slowly, pour the hot milk into the egg mixture while whisking continuously to prevent the eggs from scrambling. Return the mixture to the saucepan and place over low heat, stirring frequently, until the custard thinly coats the back of a wooden spoon. Do not let boil.

3. Pour back into the bowl and set aside for about 30 minutes, stirring occasionally, until cooled to room temperature. For more rapid chilling, fill a sink halfway with cold water and ice and place the bowl of mixture in it for 20 minutes. Never put the hot mixture into the refrigerator.

4. Once cooled, cover the mixture and refrigerate, ideally overnight, but at least for 6 hours, until thoroughly chilled (at least 40°F).

5. Remove the vanilla bean and pour the mixture into an ice cream machine. Churn according to the manufacturer's instructions. If making by hand, see the instructions on page 15.

6. When the churning is completed, use a spoon or spatula to scrape the ice cream into a freezer-proof container with a lid (to protect the ice cream from surface frosting in the freezer). Freeze until it reaches the correct scooping texture (at least 2 hours). You can rinse and dry vanilla beans after use, then store them in sugar or use them for future ice cream-making or baking recipes.

MY SEX IS ICE CREAM MARILYN MONROE

A RICH, LUXURIOUS BLEND OF FRESH CREAM INFUSED WITH EXOTIC BLACK PEARLS
FROM THE MADAGASCAN VANILLA BEAN

Inside scoop

USED IN » THE CRYBABY PAGE 110

PRISCILLA CREAM OF THE DESSERT
WHITE CHOCOLATE ICE CREAM

INSPIRED BY THE TRULY WONDROUS STAGE SHOW, WE LAUNCHED THE WORLD'S FIRST GAY ICE CREAM BAR POP-UP, QUEENS OF THE DESSERT. IN THIS DEN OF DEBAUCHERY IN COVENT GARDEN, LONDON, WE INVITED GUESTS TO SADDLE UP FOR SORDID SUNDAES WHILE IN THE WINDOW ICE CREAM POLE DANCER, "MR. WHIPPY," WHIPPED UP A STORM, AND VICE CREAM MASSEUR "JORGE OF THE JUNGLE" OFFERED COMPLEMENTARY ICE CREAM FACIALS AND BODY MASSAGES. WE CREATED A RETRO-COOL CABARET OF CROSS-DRESSING FLAVORS TO COMPLEMENT THE THEME. CAMPER THAN A ROW OF PINK TENTS FILLED WITH OODLES OF DOUBLE ENTENDRE, THIS WHITE CHOCOLATE ICE CREAM DOESN'T DRAG, IT SINGS.

· 1 cup whole milk · ½ cup heavy cream · 2 egg yolks · ⅓ cup plus 1 tablespoon superfine or granulated sugar · pinch of sea salt · 4 ounces white chocolate · 2 heaping teaspoons malted milk powder · 2–3 capfuls Irish cream liqueur (such as Baileys)

1. Pour the milk and cream into a large saucepan and heat gently, stirring occasionally, until the mixture begins to steam but not boil.

2. Meanwhile, whisk the egg yolks in a heatproof bowl until smooth. Add the sugar and salt and whisk until pale and slightly fluffy.

3. Gradually and slowly, pour the hot milk into the egg mixture while whisking continuously to prevent the eggs from scrambling. Return the mixture to the saucepan and place over low heat, stirring frequently, until the custard thinly coats the back of a wooden spoon. Do not let boil.

4. Melt the chocolate in a double boiler or a heatproof bowl set over a saucepan of simmering water. Pour it into the warm custard along with the malted milk powder and Irish cream, strring well. Pour the mixture back into the bowl and set aside for about 30 minutes, stirring occasionally, until cooled to room temperature. For more rapid chilling, fill a sink halfway with cold water and ice and place the bowl of mixture in it for 20 minutes.

5. Once cooled, cover the mixture and refrigerate, ideally overnight, but at least for 6 hours, until thoroughly chilled (at least 40°F). Pour the chilled mixture into an ice cream machine and churn according to the manufacturer's instructions. If making by hand, see the instructions on page 15.

6. When the churning is completed, use a spoon or spatula to scrape the ice cream into a freezer-proof container with a lid. Freeze until it reaches the correct scooping texture (at least 2 hours).

Inside scoop VIRGINAL WHITE STICKY CHOCOLATE SHOT THROUGH WITH A SUBLIMINAL ZAP OF MALTED MILK, VIOLATED WITH A SPLASH OF IRISH CREAM LIQUEUR

USED IN ≫ NUCLEAR WINTER PAGE 136

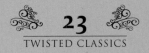
CHOC AND AWE
DARK CHOCOLATE ICE CREAM

MAKE ICE CREAM NOT WAR. WITH THIS INTENSE CHOCOLATE ICE CREAM THAT RUNS LIKE A MIND-MELTING MELODY. RIFFING ON 70 PERCENT COCOA NOTES, STRONG, EARTHY FRUIT TONES AND A VELVETY MOUTHFEEL, IT WILL SATIATE YOUR DARKEST DESIRES AND TRANSPORT ADDICTS TO CHOCOLATE NIRVANA. EACH TYPE OF CHOCOLATE IMPARTS ITS OWN FLAVOR STAMP BASED ON ITS PROVENANCE. WE USE VENEZUELAN, ECUADOREAN, AND SOMETIMES GHANAIAN CHOCOLATE.

· **1 cup whole milk** · **½ cup heavy cream** · **2 egg yolks** · **⅓ cup plus 1 tablespoon superfine or granulated sugar** · **½ cup plus 1 tablespoon unsweetened cocoa powder** · **5 ounces bittersweet chocolate (at least 70 percent cocoa solids), finely chopped**

1. Pour the milk and cream into a large saucepan and heat gently, stirring occasionally, until the mixture begins to steam but not boil.

2. Meanwhile, whisk the egg yolks in a heatproof bowl until smooth. Add the superfine sugar and whisk until pale and slightly fluffy.

3. Take the milk off the heat and whisk in the cocoa powder. Add the chocolate and stir until completely melted. Gradually and slowly, pour the chocolate milk into the egg mixture while whisking continuously to prevent the eggs from scrambling. Return the mixture to the saucepan and place over low heat, stirring frequently, until the custard thinly coats the back of a wooden spoon. Do not let boil.

4. Pour the mixture back into the bowl and set aside for about 30 minutes, stirring occasionally, until cooled to room temperature. For more rapid chilling, fill a sink halfway with cold water and ice and place the bowl of mixture in it for 20 minutes. Never put the hot mixture into the refrigerator.

5. Once cooled, cover the mixture and refrigerate, ideally overnight, but at least for 6 hours, until thoroughly chilled (at least 40°F). Pour the chilled mixture into an ice cream machine and churn according to the manufacturer's instructions. If making by hand, see the instructions on page 15.

6. When the churning is completed, use a spoon or spatula to scrape the ice cream into a freezer-proof container with a lid. Freeze until it reaches the correct scooping texture (at least 2 hours).

I SCOOP, THEREFORE I AM

A THUNDERING ASSAULT ON THE SENSES, THIS RICH, CHOCOLATE GANACHE-STYLE ICE CREAM DELIVERS A THRILLING BLITZKRIEG OF COCOA KICKS

USED IN ≫ THE FEDERICI

Y

PAGE 140

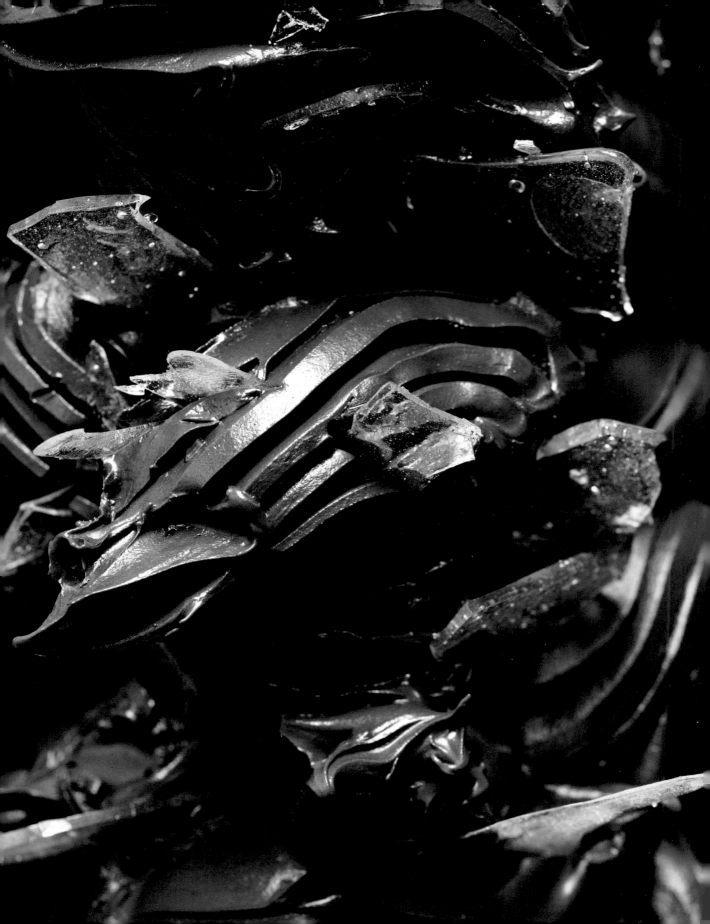

SEX, DRUGS, AND CHOC 'N' ROLL

MILK CHOCOLATE ICE CREAM

FIGHT FOR YOUR RIGHT TO SELF-MEDICATE WITH THE NATION'S FAVORITE NARCOTIC. THIS MILD, ELEGANT, CREAMY RECIPE HAS AN EDGY SEA SALT HINT THAT ELEVATES A COMFORTING MILKY MOMENT INTO SOMETHING MORE WONKY THAN WONKA. TO PARAPHRASE THE WORDS OF THE SINGER IAN DURY—HIT ME WITH YOUR LICKING STICK, HIT ME, HIT ME.

• 1 cup whole milk • ½ cup heavy cream • 2 egg yolks • ⅓ cup plus 1 tablespoon superfine or granulated sugar • pinch sea salt • ¼ cup unsweetened cocoa powder
• 4 ounces milk chocolate, finely chopped, plus extra for sprinkles

1. Pour the milk and cream into a large saucepan and heat gently, stirring occasionally, until the mixture begins to steam but not boil.

2. Meanwhile, whisk the egg yolks in a heatproof bowl until smooth. Add the superfine sugar and salt and whisk until pale and slightly fluffy.

3. Take the milk off the heat and whisk in the cocoa powder. Add the chocolate and stir until completely melted. Gradually and slowly, pour the chocolate milk into the egg mixture while whisking continuously to prevent the eggs from scrambling. Return the mixture to the saucepan and place over low heat, stirring frequently, until the custard thinly coats the back of a wooden spoon. Do not let boil.

4. Pour the mixture back into the bowl and set aside for about 30 minutes, stirring occasionally, until cooled to room temperature. For more rapid chilling, fill a sink halfway with

cold water and ice and place the bowl of mixture in it for 20 minutes. Never put the hot mixture into the refrigerator.

5. Once cooled, cover the mixture and refrigerate, ideally overnight, but at least for 6 hours, until thoroughly chilled (at least 40°F). Pour the chilled mixture into an ice cream machine and churn according to the manufacturer's instructions. If making by hand, see the instructions on page 15.

6. When the churning is completed, use a spoon or spatula to scrape the ice cream into a freezer-proof container with a lid. Freeze until it reaches the correct scooping texture (at least 2 hours). Use a cheese slicer or grater to make chocolate sprinkles to decorate.

ANARCHY … WITH SPRINKLES

A DELIRIOUS CREAM TEASE OF BUTTERY COCOA NOTES

Inside scoop

USED IN

≫

THE JUGGERNAUT
PAGE 128

A CHOCWORK ORANGE

DARK CHOCOLATE & ORANGE

THE ICECREAMISTS ARE MORE SID AND NANCY THAN BEN AND JERRY. SO OUR FOCUS GROUPS ARE MORE LIKE SUBVERSIVE INTERROGATIONS. WE BLINDFOLDED 40 OF OUR FANS AND SUBJECTED THEM TO AN EXTREME ICE CREAM TASTING. THE FIRST FLAVOR WE TRIED WAS THIS BITTERSWEET ORGY OF DECADENT COCOA AND ORANGE. ON THE BASIS OF THE RESPONSES, WE HAVE ENOUGH EVIDENCE TO PLACE THIS ICE CREAM ON AN ASSAULT CHARGE.

· 1 cup whole milk · ½ cup heavy cream · 2 egg yolks · ⅓ cup plus 1 tablespoon superfine or granulated sugar · ½ cup plus 1 tablespoon cocoa powder · 5 ounces bittersweet chocolate (at least 70 percent cocoa solids), finely chopped · ¼ cup orange extract, or to taste · zest of ½ an orange, to decorate

1. Pour the milk and cream into a large saucepan and heat gently, stirring occasionally, until the mixture begins to steam but not boil.

2. Meanwhile, whisk the egg yolks in a heatproof bowl until smooth. Add the superfine sugar and whisk until pale and slightly fluffy.

3. Take the milk off the heat and whisk in the cocoa powder. Add the chocolate and orange extract and stir until completely melted. Gradually and slowly, pour the chocolate milk into the egg mixture while whisking continuously to prevent the eggs from scrambling. Return the mixture to the saucepan and place over low heat, stirring frequently, until the custard thinly coats the back of a wooden spoon. Do not let boil.

4. Pour the mixture back into the bowl and set aside for about 30 minutes, stirring occasionally, until cooled to room temperature. For more rapid chilling, fill a sink halfway with cold water and ice and place the bowl of mixture in it for 20 minutes. Never put the hot mixture into the refrigerator.

5. Once cooled, cover the mixture and refrigerate, ideally overnight, but at least for 6 hours, until thoroughly chilled (at least 40°F). Pour the chilled mixture into an ice cream machine and churn according to the manufacturer's instructions. If making by hand, see the instructions on page 15.

6. When the churning is completed, use a spoon or spatula to scrape the ice cream into a freezer-proof container with a lid. Freeze until it reaches the correct scooping texture (at least 2 hours).

7. Decorate each portion with orange zest before serving.

GINGIANA JONES
ASIAN SPICED GINGER ICE CREAM

A WHIP-CRACKING MIX OF GROUND GINGER, SYRUP-RICH PRESERVED GINGER, AND CRYSTALLIZED GINGER THAT COMBINES EASTERN HEAT WITH COOLING CREAM. DON'T BE DECEIVED BY ITS MATURE APPEARANCE, THIS ICE CREAM WILL STALK YOU, THEN GRIP YOU BY YOUR THROAT LIKE THE INSIDIOUS FU MANCHU, BEFORE THROWING YOU ON THE FLOOR AND DELIVERING A VISCERAL SMACK OF HEAT TO YOUR CHOPS. HEE-YA!

• 1 cup whole milk • ½ cup heavy cream • 2 egg yolks • ⅓ cup plus 1 tablespoon superfine or granulated sugar • 1½ heaping tablespoons ground ginger • 3 balls of preserved ginger • 1 tablespoon preserved ginger syrup • ⅔ cup finely chopped crystallized ginger, plus extra to decorate

1. Pour the milk and cream into a large saucepan and heat gently, stirring occasionally, until the mixture begins to steam but not boil.

2. Meanwhile, whisk the egg yolks in a heatproof bowl until smooth. Add the sugar and whisk until pale and slightly fluffy. Gradually and slowly, pour the hot milk into the egg mixture while whisking continuously to prevent the eggs from scrambling. Return the mixture to the saucepan and place over low heat, stirring frequently, until the custard thinly coats the back of a wooden spoon. Do not let boil.

3. Add the ground ginger, preserved ginger and syrup and mix using an immersionblender. Pour the mixture back into the bowl and set aside for about 30 minutes, stirring occasionally, until cooled to room temperature. For more rapid chilling, fill a sink halfway with cold water and ice and place the bowl of mixture in it for 20 minutes. Never put the hot mixture into the refrigerator.

4. Once cooled, cover the mixture and refrigerate, ideally overnight, but at least for 6 hours, until thoroughly chilled (at least 15°5F). Pour the chilled mixture into an ice cream machine and churn according to the manufacturer's instructions. If making by hand, see the instructions on page 15.

5. When the churning is completed, fold the crystallized ginger into the ice cream, then use a spoon or spatula to scrape the mixture into a freezer-proof container with a lid. Freeze until it reaches the correct scooping texture (at least 2 hours).

6. Decorate each serving with some finely chopped crystallized ginger.

GET YOUR KICKS WITH OUR LICKS

SET LIGHT TO THE FUSE AND WATCH IT BURN. WONDERFULLY OFFSET BY THE SUGARY AMALGAM OF CYSTALLIZED GINGER.

Inside scoop

TAKING THE PISTACCHIO

PISTACCHIO ICE CREAM

WHILE YOU CAN SOURCE GREAT PISTACCHIOS FROM IRAN AND ITALY, THE BEST IN THE WORLD ARE THE "GREEN GOLD" OF SICILY, FROM THE PISTACCHIO CAPITAL OF BRONTE. GROWN ON THE LAVA SOIL OF MOUNT ETNA, THESE SMOKY, OCHER-GREEN JEWELS CARRY A SWEET, DELICATE AROMA THAT CAN RENDER THE MOST OUTSPOKEN AFICIONADO SPEECHLESS IN A MAFIOSO-STYLE CODE OF SILENCE. SICILIANS CURIOUSLY ALLEGE THAT THE PISTACCHIO CAN "EXCITE THE ARDORS OF VENUS AND INCREASE THE FEMININE HUMOR." FOR US, IT'S THE ULTIMATE NUT JOB. FOR A TOTALLY NUTTY TWIST, YOU CAN REPLACE THE PISTACCHIOS WITH HAZELNUTS.

· 1 cup whole milk · ½ cup heavy cream · 2 egg yolks
· ⅓ cup plus 1 tablespoon superfine or granulated sugar · pinch of sea salt
· 1 cup shelled, unsalted pistacchio nuts, plus a few extra to decorate
· dash of almond extract (about ¼ teaspoon)

1. Preheat your oven to 300°F. Spread ¾ cup of the pistacchios on a baking pan and place in the oven for 10 minutes, until lightly browned. This will release locked-in flavor. Let cool a little, then put into a coffee grinder or food processor and grind to a fine powder. Transfer to a small bowl, add the almond extract, and mix well.

2. Pour the milk and cream into a large saucepan and heat gently, stirring occasionally, until the mixture begins to steam but not boil. Meanwhile, whisk the egg yolks in a heatproof bowl until smooth. Add the sugar and salt and whisk until pale and slightly fluffy. Gradually and slowly, pour the hot milk into the egg mixture while whisking continuously to prevent the eggs from scrambling.

3. Return the mixture to the saucepan and place over low heat. Add the pistacchio powder and cook, stirring frequently, until the custard thinly coats the back of a wooden spoon. Do not let boil. While hot, blend the mixture thoroughly with an immersion blender. Strain into a bowl—once through a fine

strainer, and then through a cheesecloth to remove all the nut pieces but retain the flavor, then stir in the almond extract.

4. Set aside for about 30 minutes, stirring occasionally, until cooled to room temperature. For more rapid chilling, fill a sink halfway with cold water and ice and place the bowl of mixture in it for 20 minutes. Never put the hot mixture into the refrigerator.

5. Once cooled, cover the mixture and refrigerate, ideally overnight, but at least for 6 hours, until thoroughly chilled (at least 40°F). Pour the chilled mixture into an ice cream machine and churn according to the manufacturer's instructions. If making by hand, see the instructions on page 15.

6. When the churning is completed, chop the remaining pistacchios and fold into the ice cream. Use a spoon or spatula to scrape the ice cream into a freezer-proof container with a lid and freeze until it reaches the correct scooping texture (at least 2 hours).

7. Decorate each serving with chopped pistacchios.

A POETICALLY BALANCED ICE CREAM WITH WONDERFUL NUTTY NOTES THAT WILL
LEAVE YOU REACHING FOR YOUR THESAURUS

Inside scoop

USED IN ⟫ THE OMERTA

PAGE 111

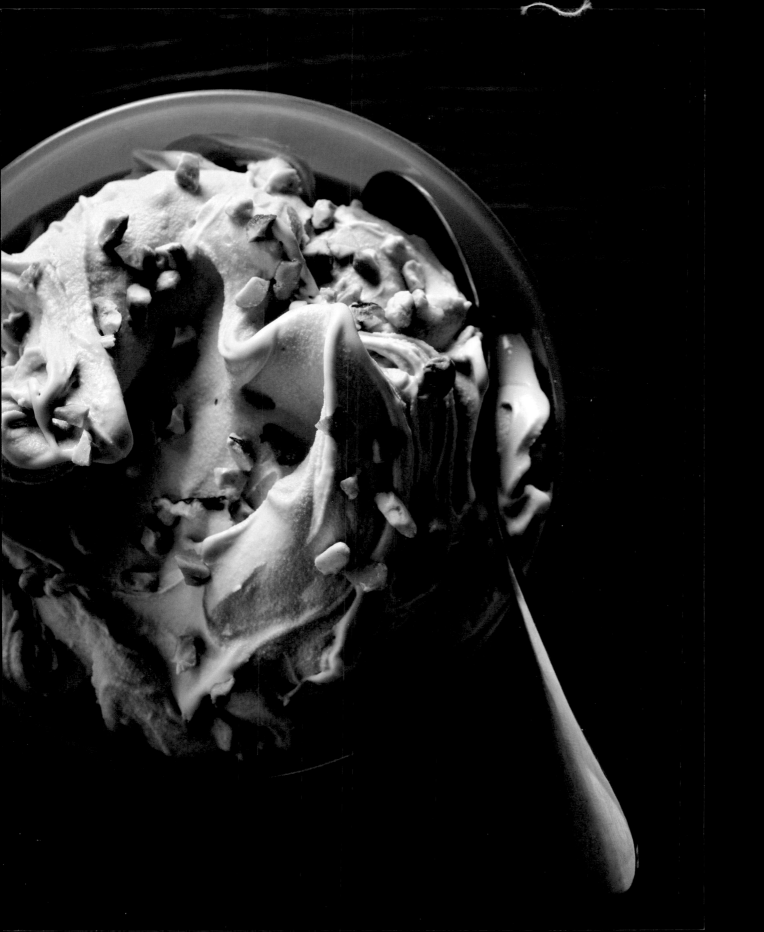

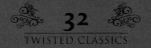
NUTS ABOUT CHOCLAND YARD

HAZELNUT CHOCOLATE ICE CREAM

I WAS BANNED FROM ENTERING LONDON DURING THE STATE OPENING OF PARLIAMENT IN 2005, ON THE GROUNDS THAT THE METROPOLITAN POLICE COULD NOT "GUARANTEE" MY SAFETY, SO I STAYED AT HOME AND MADE THIS ICE CREAM INSTEAD. DESCRIBED BY MY ARRESTING OFFICERS AS A CURFEW-BREAKING BLEND OF CREAM AND HAZELNUT CHOCOLATE THAT WOULD BE USED IN EVIDENCE AGAINST ME. DO I LOVE THIS ICE CREAM? GUILTY AS CHARGED, YOUR HONOR.

· **1 cup whole milk** · **½ cup heavy cream** · **2 egg yolks**
· **⅓ cup plus 1 tablespoon sugar** · **¾ cup hazelnut-chocolate spread (such as Nutella)**

1. Pour the milk and cream into a large saucepan and heat gently, stirring occasionally, until the mixture begins to steam but not boil.

2. Meanwhile, whisk the egg yolks in a heatproof bowl until smooth. Add the superfine sugar and whisk until pale and slightly fluffy.

3. Take the milk off the heat and whisk in the hazelnut-chocolate spread until blended. Gradually and slowly, pour the chocolate milk into the egg mixture while whisking continuously to prevent the eggs from scrambling. Return the mixture to the saucepan and place over low heat, stirring frequently, until the custard thinly coats the back of a wooden spoon. Do not let boil.

4. Pour the mixture back into the bowl and set aside for about 30 minutes, stirring occasionally, until cooled to room temperature. For more rapid chilling, fill a sink halfway with cold water and ice and place the bowl of mixture in it for 20 minutes. Never put the hot mixture into the refrigerator.

5. Once cooled, cover the mixture and refrigerate, ideally overnight, but at least for 6 hours, until thoroughly chilled (at least 40°F). Pour the chilled mixture into an ice cream machine and churn according to the manufacturer's instructions. If making by hand, see the instructions on page 15.

6. When the churning is completed, use a spoon or spatula to scrape the ice cream into a freezer-proof container with a lid. Freeze until it reaches the correct scooping texture (at least 2 hours).

7. To create a great chocolate sauce, place ⅓ cup of Nutella in a heatproof bowl and microwave for 60 seconds on medium, stirring every 20 seconds, then pour the sauce over your ice cream. Bellissimo!

PUT YOUR CLOTHES ON AND I'LL BUY YOU AN ICE CREAM JAMES BOND

Inside scoop THE BASIS FOR NUTELLA IS GIANDUIA, A CHOCOLATE AND HAZELNUT CONCOCTION CREATED IN TURIN, WHICH BECAME POPULAR DURING WORLD WAR II WHEN COCOA WAS IN SHORT SUPPLY AND HAZELNUT PASTE WAS USED AS A SUBSTITUTE.

CARAMELTDOWN
DULCE DE LECHE ICE CREAM

YOU'RE IN THE MIDDLE OF A TWENTY-FIRST-CENTURY MELTDOWN: YOUR BANK IS BUST AND THE ATM MACHINES ARE EMPTY. FEAR NOT, BECAUSE IN A TIME OF ADVERSITY LIES OPPORTUNITY, IN THIS CASE, THE CARAMELTDOWN—A WARM, SILKY CUSTARD BASE WITH DULCE DE LECHE, AN ARGENTINE BUTTERSCOTCH-"CONDENSED-MILK"-CARAMEL-CHEW KICK. THIS SEDUCTIVE ORAL LUBRICANT WILL LEAVE YOU DEFROSTING HELPLESSLY IN A PUDDLE ON THE FLOOR AS THE WORLD COLLAPSES AROUND YOU. DON'T CRY FOR ME ARGENTINA? IT'LL BE THE REST OF THE WORLD THAT'S REACHING FOR THE TISSUES AFTER YOU'VE LICKED THIS NUMBER.

• 1 cup milk • ½ cup heavy cream • 2 egg yolks •
• ⅓ cup plus 1 tablespoon superfine or granulated sugar • large pinch of sea salt •
• 1 cup Dulce de Leche sauce (see page 154), plus a little extra for drizzling •

1. Pour the milk and cream into a large saucepan and heat gently, stirring occasionally, until the mixture begins to steam but not boil.

2. Meanwhile, whisk the egg yolks in a heatproof bowl until smooth. Add the sugar and salt and whisk until pale and slightly fluffy. Gradually and slowly, pour the hot milk into the egg mixture while whisking continuously to prevent the eggs from scrambling. Return the mixture to the saucepan and place over low heat, stirring frequently until the custard thinly coats the back of a wooden spoon. Do not let boil.

3. Pour back into the bowl and set aside for about 30 minutes, stirring occasionally, until cooled to room temperature. For more rapid chilling, fill a sink halfway with cold water and ice and place the bowl of mixture in it for 20 minutes. Never put the hot mixture into the refrigerator.

4. Once cooled, cover the mixture and refrigerate, ideally overnight, but at least for 6 hours, until thoroughly chilled (at least 40°5).

5. Add ½ cup of the Dulce de Leche sauce to the chilled mixture and combine well with an immersion blender. Pour into an ice cream machine and churn according to the manufacturer's instructions. If making by hand, see the instructions on page 15.

6. Just before the churning is finished, warm another ½ cup of the sauce in a heatproof bowl and microwave on medium for 20–30 seconds to loosen. Gradually pour the sauce into the ice cream for the last 2 minutes of churning. When the churning is completed, use a spoon or spatula to scrape the ice cream into a freezer-proof container with a lid. Freeze until it reaches the correct scooping texture (at least 2 hours).

7. Drizzle each serving with a little extra sauce, gently warmed.

CAPITALISM SUCKS

Inside scoop

DULCE DE LECHE MEANS "SWEET MILK" AND IT IS PREPARED BY SLOWLY HEATING SWEETENED MILK TO CREATE A CARAMELIZED SUGAR FLAVOR THAT IS FIENDISHLY SEDUCTIVE

USED IN ≫ MOLOTOFFEE

PAGE 120

THE CUSTARDY SUITE
TRADITIONAL ITALIAN CREMA ICE CREAM

DURING MY TIME AT THE UNIVERSITY OF ADVERSITY, I'VE BEEN BOILED, SCRAMBLED, POACHED, AND FRIED IN MANY A CUSTODY SUITE BY OVERENTHUSIASTIC LAW ENFORCMENT OFFICERS. THIS ICE CREAM, A TRADITIONAL ITALIAN CREMA, IS ANOTHER ARRESTING EXPERIENCE THAT WILL LEAVE DEFENDANTS DIALLING 911 TO CONFESS TO A REPEAT OFFENSE. IT IS AN EGGIER VARIATION OF OUR BASE MIX, AND ALL THE MORE DELICIOUS FOR IT. UNADULTERATED EGGSTACY!

- 1 cup whole milk • ½ cup heavy cream • 4 egg yolks
- ⅓ cup plus 1 tablespoon sugar • pinch of sea salt

1. Pour the milk and cream into a large saucepan and heat gently, stirring occasionally, until the mixture begins to steam but not boil.

2. Meanwhile, whisk the egg yolks in a heatproof bowl until smooth. Add the sugar and salt and whisk until pale and slightly fluffy. Gradually and slowly, pour the hot milk into the egg mixture while whisking continuously to prevent the eggs from scrambling. Return the mixture to the saucepan and place over low heat, stirring frequently until the custard thinly coats the back of a wooden spoon. Do not let boil.

3. Pour back into the bowl and set aside for about 30 minutes, stirring occasionally, until cooled to room temperature. For more rapid chilling, fill a sink halfway with cold water and ice and place the bowl of mixture in it for 20 minutes. Never put the hot mixture into the refrigerator.

4. Once cooled, cover the mixture and refrigerate, ideally overnight, but at least for 6 hours, until thoroughly chilled (at least 40°F). Pour the chilled mixture into an ice cream machine and churn according to the manufacturer's instructions. If making by hand, see the instructions on page 15.

5. When the churning is completed, use a spoon or spatula to scrape the ice cream into a freezer-proof container with a lid. Freeze until it reaches the correct scooping texture (at least 2 hours).

GOD SAVE THE CREAM

AN INTENSELY RICH, CUSTARDY FLAVOR WITH A THICK, LUSTROUS MOUTHFEEL

Inside scoop

USED IN ≫ MANTECATO ITALIANO
PAGE 138

DESSERT STORM
TIRAMISU ICE CREAM

MY WIFE NADINE AND I ARRIVED FOR OUR NUPTIALS IN AN ICE CREAM VAN EMBLAZONED WITH THE BANNER "WEDLOCKED: THERE ARE SOME INSTITUTIONS YOU CAN'T ESCAPE FROM." THE NIGHT OF THE WEDDING, MY BROTHER DAVID AND I DISCUSSED THE MERITS OF A TIRAMISU ICE CREAM AND DECIDED IT WAS THE ULTIMATE D ESSERT STORM, BUT WHAT WAS THE PERFECT COMBO OF INGREDIENTS? MORE MARSALA WINE? SAVOIARDI LADYFINGERS? AS THE DEBATE RAGED INTO THE NIGHT, I TOLD MY INCREASINGLY IMPATIENT WIFE, "I'LL BE AT THE MARITAL SUITE BY 11:30 P.M. IF I'M LATE, START WITHOUT ME."

• 1 cup whole milk • ½ cup heavy cream • 2 egg yolks
• ⅓ cup plus 1 tablespoon firmly packed brown sugar • pinch of sea salt • 4 ladyfingers, preferably Savoiardi • ⅓ cup mascarpone cheese • ⅔ cup Marsala wine
• 1 capful Kahlua liqueur • 1 capful dark rum • unsweetened cocoa powder, to dust

FOR THE SYRUP • ½ cup granulated sugar • 1 heaping tablespoon instant coffee granules

1. Pour the milk and cream into a large saucepan and heat gently, stirring occasionally, until the mixture begins to steam but not boil.

2. Meanwhile, whisk the egg yolks in a heatproof bowl until smooth. Add the sugar and salt and whisk until slightly fluffy. Gradually and slowly, pour the hot milk into the egg mixture while whisking continuously to prevent the eggs from scrambling. Return the mixture to the saucepan and place over low heat, stirring frequently until the custard thinly coats the back of a wooden spoon. Do not let boil.

3. Pour back into the bowl and set aside for about 30 minutes, stirring occasionally, until cooled to room temperature. For more rapid chilling, fill a sink halfway with cold water and ice and place the bowl of mixture in it for 20 minutes. Never put the hot mixture into the refrigerator. Once cooled, cover the mixture and refrigerate, ideally overnight, but at least for 6 hours, until thoroughly chilled (at least 40°F).

4. Meanwhile, make the syrup. Put the granulated sugar and ½ cup water into a saucepan and whisk over low heat until the sugar dissolves. Add the coffee granules and simmer while whisking, until the liquid turns into a syrup.

5. Put the ladyfingers on a plate and drizzle the syrup over them. Set aside.

6. Using a spoon, fold the mascarpone into the cold custard, then stir in the Marsala. Pour the mixture into an ice cream machine, add the Kahlua and rum, and churn according to manufacturer's instructions. If making by hand, see the instructions on page 15.

7. When the churning is completed, use a spoon or spatula to scrape the ice cream into a freezer-proof container, topping the ice cream with one layer of syrupy ladyfingers. Dust with cocoa powder, place the lid on, and freeze until it reaches the correct scooping texture (at least 2 hours).

8. Lightly dust each portion with cocoa powder before serving.

TIRAMISU IS ITALIAN FOR "PICK ME UP." THIS SUBZERO INTERPRETATION ISN'T ANY OLD PICK-ME-UP—IT'S AN INTERNATIONAL ABDUCTION!

Inside scoop

LIVING IN CINNAMON
APPLE AND CINNAMON ICE CREAM

AS OSCAR WILDE ONCE SAID, "I CAN RESIST EVERYTHING EXCEPT TEMPTATION." IN THIS CASE, A FRENCH TOPLESS MODEL AND CONSEQUENT "DEPLORABLE ATTENDANCE RECORD" RESULTING IN MY EXPULSION FROM ART COLLEGE. SUCH WERE THE EDUCATIONAL DISTRACTIONS OF LIVING IN SIN. HER FATHER, PATRICK, WHO LIVED IN PARIS AND RAN A MAGAZINE FOR THE ASSOCIATION OF BARMEN IN FRANCE, INITIATED ME INTO THE ART OF DECADENCE, CULTIVATING MY TASTE FOR MONTECRISTO CIGARS, FINE ARMAGNAC, AND SEDUCTIVE SPICES, SUCH AS CINNAMON...

- 1 cup whole milk · ½ cup heavy cream · 2 egg yolks
- ⅓ cup plus 1 tablespoon superfine or granulated sugar · ⅓ cup applesauce
- 2 teaspoons ground cinnamon , plus extra for dusting
- ½ cup balsamic vinegar (optional)

1. Pour the milk and cream into a large saucepan and heat gently, stirring occasionally, until the mixture begins to steam but not boil.

2. Meanwhile, whisk the egg yolks in a heatproof bowl until smooth. Add the sugar and whisk until pale and slightly fluffy. Gradually and slowly, pour the hot milk into the egg mixture while whisking continuously to prevent the eggs from scrambling. Return the mixture to the saucepan and place over low heat, stirring frequently, until the custard thinly coats the back of a wooden spoon. Do not let boil.

3. Pour back into the bowl and set aside for about 30 minutes, stirring occasionally, until cooled to room temperature. For more rapid chilling, fill a sink halfway with cold water and ice and place the bowl of mixture in it for 20 minutes. Never put the hot mixture into the refrigerator.

4. Once cooled, cover the mixture and refrigerate, ideally overnight, but at least for 6 hours, until thoroughly chilled (at least 40°F).

5. Add the applesauce and cinnamon to the chilled mixture and combine well with an immersion blender. Pour into an ice cream machine and churn according to the manufacturer's instructions. If making by hand, see the instructions on page 15.

6. When the churning is completed, gradually fold in the balsamic (if using). Use a spoon or spatula to scrape the ice cream into a freezer-proof container with a lid, then freeze until it reaches the correct scooping texture (at least 2 hours).

7. Dust each portion with extra cinnamon before serving.

GIVE IT A SWIRL

THIS IS A POETIC COMBINATION OF TART APPLE, OFFSET BY A BITTERSWEET SMIDGEN OF NORTH AFRICAN CINNAMON AND A DASH OF SUGAR

Inside scoop

SCARLETT FEVER

STRAWBERRY AND BALSAMIC ICE CREAM

BLESSED ARE THE LIPS OF THE ACTRESS SCARLETT JOHANSSON—A ONE-WOMAN WARM FRONT WITH A SMOLDERING, FULL-BODIED POUT THAT COULD MAKE A LOLLIPOP TOO HAPPY. NOW, YOU MAY BE THINKING HOW DOES SCARLETT RELATE TO STRAWBERRIES? FOR SOME PERVERSE PSYCHOLOGICAL REASONING KNOWN ONLY TO MY PSYCHIATRIST, A GREAT-LOOKING STRAWBERRY REMINDED ME OF THE FRUITIEST SMACKERS IN THE WORLD. WE DEDICATE THIS ICE CREAM TO HER, SO PUCKER UP FOR A DOSE OF SCARLETT FEVER.

• 1 cup whole milk • ½ cup heavy cream • 2 egg yolks
• ⅓ cup superfine or granulated sugar • FOR THE STRAWBERRY SYRUP • 1¼ cups hulled and chopped strawberries • ⅓ cup superfine or granulated sugar • juice of ½ a lemon
FOR THE BALSAMIC REDUCTION • ½ cup balsamic vinegar • superfine or granulated sugar, to taste

1. First make the syrup. Put all the syrup ingredients into a saucepan and place over low heat until simmering gently and the strawberries are softening. Simmer for about 5 minutes, stirring occasionally, then pour into a heatproof bowl.

2. Fill a sink halfway with cold water and ice and place the bowl of syrup in it for 20 minutes. Never put the hot mixture into the refrigerator. Once cooled, cover the syrup and refrigerate, ideally overnight, but at least for 6 hours, until thoroughly chilled (at least 40°F).

3. Pour the milk and cream into a large saucepan and heat gently, stirring occasionally, until it begins to steam but not boil.

4. Meanwhile, whisk the egg yolks in a heatproof bowl until smooth. Add the sugar and whisk until pale and slightly fluffy. Gradually and slowly, pour the hot milk into the egg mixture while whisking continuously to prevent the eggs from scrambling. Return the mixture to the saucepan and place over low heat, stirring frequently, until the custard thinly coats the back of a wooden spoon. Do not let boil.

5. Pour back into the bowl and set aside for about 30 minutes, stirring occasionally, until cooled to room temperature. For

more rapid chilling, fill a sink halfway with cold water and ice and place the bowl of mixture in it for 20 minutes. Never put the hot mixture into the refrigerator. Once cooled, cover and refrigerate, ideally overnight, but at least for 6 hours, until thoroughly chilled (at least 40°F).

6. Using a spoon, stir three-quarters of the syrup into the chilled mixture; do not use a blender because you want to retain the texture of the strawberry pieces. Pour into an ice cream machine and churn according to the manufacturer's instructions, adding the remainder of the strawberry syrup about 5 minutes before the end. If making by hand, see the instructions on page 15.

7. When the churning is completed, use a spoon or spatula to scrape the ice cream into a freezer-proof container with a lid. Freeze until it reaches scooping texture (at least 2 hours).

8. Meanwhile, put the balsamic vinegar into a saucepan on moderate heat and whisk briskly until it reduces by about half and becomes syrupy. Add a little sugar to taste, if required.

9. Offer the reduction with the ice cream: the seemingly odd combo of balsamic and strawberry works well together.

WE MEAN EVERY SYLLABLE WHEN WE SAY THIS IS A SEDUCTIVE COMBO OF FRESH
CREAM CUT THROUGH WITH ZINGY STRAWBERRY FLAVOR.

Inside scoop DEFINITELY NOT JUST LIP SERVICE...

USED IN ≫

STRAWBERRY ICE QUAKE

PAGE 126

MINT CONDITION
MINT CHOCOLATE ICE CREAM

ONCE UPON A TIME ON ST. GEORGE'S DAY, SCOTTISH POLICE WERE FORCED TO SURROUND A MOUNTAIN PEAK AFTER RUMORS CIRCULATED THAT I PLANNED TO MARK THE DAY BY PLANTING THE CROSS OF ST. GEORGE ON BEN NEVIS PEAK WHILE DRESSED IN A SUIT OF ARMOR. AS ANY FOOL COULD HAVE TOLD YOU, I WASN'T IN MINT CONDITION. I WOULD HAVE STRUGGLED TO SCALE A TOILET IN THAT GETUP, LET ALONE CLIMB A MOUNTAIN. ONE OF THE BEST THINGS I DISCOVERED ABOUT SCOTLAND IN MY TRAVAILS WAS THEIR LOVE OF MINTS. I CAME ACROSS THIS ICE CREAM IDEA IN A SMALL PARLOR ON THE WEST COAST OF SCOTLAND— MASHED-UP AFTER-DINNER CHOCOLATE MINTS IN A DELICIOUS GOOEY, SUGARY RIPPLE, CUT THROUGH WITH FRESH MINT AND BITTER CHOCOLATE.

- 1 cup whole milk • ½ cup heavy cream • 2 egg yolks
- ⅓ cup plus 1 tablespoon superfine or granulated sugar
- 4 ounces dark chocolate with a soft mint filling, corasely chopped

1. Pour the milk and cream into a large saucepan and heat gently, stirring occasionally, until the mixture begins to steam but not boil.

2. Meanwhile, whisk the egg yolks in a heatproof bowl until smooth. Add the sugar and whisk until pale and slightly fluffy. Gradually and slowly, pour the hot milk into the egg mixture while whisking continuously to prevent the eggs from scrambling. Return the mixture to the saucepan and place over low heat, stirring frequently until the custard thinly coats the back of a wooden spoon. Do not let boil.

3. Pour the mixture back into the bowl and set aside for about 30 minutes, stirring occasionally, until cooled to room temperature. For more rapid chilling, fill a sink halfway with cold water and ice and place the bowl of mixture in it for 20 minutes. Never put the hot mixture into the refrigerator. Meanwhile, melt the chopped mint chocolate in a heatproof bowl over a saucepan of simmering water.

4. Once the ice cream mixture is cooled, add the melted mint chocolate to the bowl, along with the mixture, blend with an immersion blender, and refrigerate, ideally overnight, but at least for 6 hours, until thoroughly chilled (at least 40°C). Pour the chilled mixture into an ice cream machine and churn according to the manufacturer's instructions. If making by hand, see page 15.

5. When the churning is completed, fold in the mint chocolate with a spoon or spatula, and scrape the ice cream into a freezer-proof container with a lid. Freeze until it reaches the correct scooping texture (at least 2 hours).

6. Decorate each portion with fresh mint leaves before serving.

THE ICE CREAM MAN COMETH

A DEVASTATING MIXTURE OF FRESH MINT, CREAM, AND DARK CHOCOLATE WITH A MINTY FILLING

Inside scoop

UNDER THE CHERRY SPOON

MASCARPONE AND AMARENA CHERRY ICE CREAM

NICOLA FABBRI IS THE FASHIONABLY ELEGANT PROPRIETOR OF FABBRI, PURVEYORS OF THE FINEST AMARENA CHERRIES IN THE WORLD, WHICH ARE SOLD IN ICONIC WHITE-AND-BLUE CERAMIC JARS. THIS ICE CREAM IS INSPIRED BY MY VISIT TO THEIR FACTORY IN BOLOGNA IN THE BLISTERING SUMMER HEAT OF 2009. NICOLA'S ENGLISH WAS NEVER VERY GOOD, BUT WHEN IT CAME TO BEATING THE MASS-MARKET COMPETITION, HE WAS EXTRAORDINARILY FLUENT "YES, WHEN YOU F*&K THEM, YOU TELL ME HOW HARD YOU F*&K THEM."

- 1 cup whole milk • ½ cup heavy cream • 2 egg yolks
- ⅓ cup plus 1 tablespoon superfine or granulated sugar • pinch of sea salt
- 1 cup mascarpone cheese • 1 cup Amarena cherries, plus a few extra to decorate

1. Pour the milk and cream into a large saucepan and heat gently, stirring occasionally, until the mixture begins to steam but not boil.

2. Meanwhile, whisk the egg yolks in a heatproof bowl until smooth. Add the sugar and salt and whisk until pale and slightly fluffy. Gradually and slowly, pour the hot milk into the egg mixture while whisking continuously to prevent the eggs from scrambling. Return the mixture to the saucepan and place over low heat, stirring frequently, until the custard thinly coats the back of a wooden spoon. Do not let boil.

3. Pour back into the bowl and set aside for about 30 minutes, stirring occasionally, until cooled to room temperature. For more rapid chilling, fill a sink halfway with cold water and ice and place the bowl of mixture in it for 20 minutes. Never put the hot mixture into the refrigerator.

4. Once cooled, cover the mixture and refrigerate, ideally overnight, but at least for 6 hours, until thoroughly chilled (at least 40°F).

5. Add the mascarpone to the chilled mixture and combine well with an immersion blender. Pour the mixture into an ice cream machine and churn according to the manufacturer's instructions. If making by hand, see the instructions on page 15.

6. When the churning is completed, fold in the cherries, then use a spoon or spatula to scrape the ice cream into a freezer-proof container with a lid. Freeze until it reaches the correct scooping texture (at least 2 hours).

7. Decorate each portion with a few extra cherries before serving.

THE SPOON IS MIGHTIER THAN THE KNIFE: CHANGE YOUR SILVERWARE

A SWEET, INTENSE, THICK CREAM-TYPE FLAVOR, OFFSET BY THE BITE OF THE SLIGHTLY SOUR AMARENA CHERRIES IN SYRUP

Inside scoop

JESUS CHRIST SCOOPERSTAR
FIOR DI LATTE ICE CREAM

ATTEMPTING TO CREATE A REALLY GREAT ICE CREAM IS OFTEN LIKE TRYING TO HANDCUFF LIGHTNING. THE PURITY OF A REALLY GREAT FIOR DI LATTE (FLOWER OF MILK) DEMONSTRATES THIS MORE THAN ANY OTHER ICE CREAM, WITH A FLAVOR THAT SHOWCASES JUST MILK, CREAM, SUGAR, AND A PINCH OF SEA SALT. BECAUSE OF THIS, IT BENEFITS FROM USING THE FINEST INGREDIENTS YOU CAN GET SO THAT THE FLAVORS SHINE THROUGH. WE INCLUDE IT HERE BECAUSE IT REPRESENTS THE PUREST OF TASTES AND IS ANYTHING BUT VANILLA. IT'S OUR SUPERSTAR FOR SCOOPERSTARS.

- 1 cup whole milk · ½ cup heavy cream · 2 egg yolks
- ⅓ cup plus 1 tablespoon superfine or granulated sugar · pinch of sea salt
- zest of ½ an orange or lemon, to decorate (optional)

1. Pour the milk and cream into a large saucepan and heat gently, stirring occasionally, until the mixture begins to steam but not boil.

2. Meanwhile, whisk the egg yolks in a heatproof bowl until smooth. Add the sugar and salt and whisk until pale and slightly fluffy. Gradually and slowly, pour the hot milk into the egg mixture while whisking continuously to prevent the eggs from scrambling. Return the mixture to the saucepan and place over low heat, stirring frequently, until the custard thinly coats the back of a wooden spoon. Do not let boil.

3. Pour back into the bowl and set aside for about 30 minutes, stirring occasionally, until cooled to room temperature. For more rapid chilling, fill a sink halfway with cold water and ice and place the bowl of mixture in it for 20 minutes. Never put the hot mixture into the refrigerator.

4. Once cooled, cover the mixture and refrigerate, ideally overnight, but at least for 6 hours, until thoroughly chilled (at least 40°F). Pour the chilled mixture into an ice cream machine and churn according to the manufacturer's instructions. If making by hand, see the instructions on page 15.

5. When the churning is completed, use a spoon or spatula to scrape the ice cream into a freezer-proof container with a lid. Freeze until it reaches the correct scooping texture (at least 2 hours).

6. Top each serving with a little orange or lemon zest for a summer twist.

WITH A THICK, CHEWY MOUTHFEEL, THIS IS A CLOSE RELATIVE TO BRITISH CLOTTED CREAM

Inside scoop

ESPRESSO YOURSELF

COFFEE ICE CREAM

BRING ON THE HYPERTENSION WITH THIS EYE-POPPING, VEIN-THROBBING, JAW-DROPPING, CAFFEINE-FUELLED KICK OF WEAPONS-GRADE ESPRESSO THAT WILL LEAVE YOUR GUESTS DEFIANTLY BOUNCING UP AND DOWN TOPLESS ON MINI-TRAMPOLINES OUTSIDE. IF YOU PREFER, WHY NOT STAGE YOUR OWN BUNGA-BUNGA PARTY IN A CONE WITH TWO SCOOPS, "BERLUS-CONY"-STYLE?

· 1 cup whole milk · ½ cup heavy cream · 3 to 4 heaping teaspoons good-quality instant coffee granules, to taste · 2 egg yolks · ⅓ cup plus 1 tablespoon firmly packed brown sugar · 1 capful Kahlua liqueur, plus extra for drizzling (optional)

1. Pour the milk and cream into a large saucepan, add the coffee granules, and heat gently, stirring occasionally, until the mixture begins to steam but not boil.

2. Meanwhile, whisk the egg yolks in a heatproof bowl until smooth. Add the sugar and whisk until slightly fluffy. Gradually and slowly, pour the hot milk into the egg mixture while whisking continuously to prevent the eggs from scrambling. Return the mixture to the saucepan and place over low heat, stirring frequently, until the custard thinly coats the back of a wooden spoon. Do not let boil.

3. Pour back into the bowl and set aside for about 30 minutes, stirring occasionally, until cooled to room temperature. For more rapid chilling, fill a sink halfway with cold water and ice and place the bowl of mixture in it for 20 minutes. Never put the hot mixture into the refrigerator.

4. Once cooled, cover the mixture and refrigerate, ideally overnight, but at least for 6 hours, until thoroughly chilled (at least 40°F).

5. Add the Kahlua (if using), then pour the mixture into an ice cream machine and churn according to the manufacturer's instructions. If making by hand, see the instructions on page 15.

6. When the churning is completed, use a spoon or spatula to scrape the ice cream into a freezer-proof container with a lid. Freeze until it reaches the correct scooping texture (at least 2 hours).

7. Drizzle Kahlua over each serving, if you prefer, or place a scoop of the ice cream in a hot coffee for a decadent affogato.

Inside scoop A ROBUST BLEND OF COFFEE AND CREAM WITH A SLIGHTLY BURNED FINISH AND TOBACCO NOTES. WE NORMALLY MAKE THIS WITH ESPRESSO, BUT HAVE SIMPLIFIED THE RECIPE SO IT ISN'T NECESSARY.

USED IN » THE GODFATHER PAGE 117

THE KISS

LAVENDER ICE CREAM

ATTENTION ALL YOU LADIES IN LAVENDER. AS ROXANNE SAID TO CHRISTIAN, "YOU GIVE ME MILK INSTEAD OF CREAM." THERE IS A LESSON HERE THAT SURELY A MAN OF INCOMPARABLE PANACHE, SUCH AS CYRANO DE BERGERAC, WOULD AGREE WITH: NEVER SHORTCHANGE A LADY ON INGREDIENTS. THIS ICE CREAM IS THE SOFTEST OF KISSES, ELOQUENTLY AND VIVIDLY BROUGHT TO LIFE BY THE LEGEND HIMSELF ...

- 1 cup whole milk · ½ cup heavy cream · 2 egg yolks
- ⅓ cup plus 1 tablespoon superfine or granulated sugar ·
- 4 lavender flower heads or a few drops of food-grade lavender oil
- lavender flowers, for decoration · 1 tablespoon lavender honey (optional)

1. Pour the milk and cream into a large saucepan and heat gently, stirring occasionally, until the mixture begins to steam but not boil.

2. Meanwhile, whisk the egg yolks in a heatproof bowl until smooth. Add the sugar and whisk until pale and slightly fluffy. Gradually and slowly, pour the hot milk into the egg mixture while whisking continuously to prevent the eggs from scrambling.

3. Return the mixture to the saucepan and place over low heat. Add the lavender flower heads or oil and cook, stirring frequently, until the custard thinly coats the back of a wooden spoon. Do not let boil. If using lavender flower heads, use an immersion blender to pulse the custard and release the flavor.

4. Pour the mixture back into the bowl and set aside for about 30 minutes, stirring occasionally, until cooled to room temperature. For more rapid chilling, fill a sink halfway with cold water and ice and place the bowl of mixture in it for 20 minutes. Never put the hot mixture into the refrigerator.

5. Once cooled, cover the mixture and refrigerate, ideally overnight, but at least for 6 hours, until thoroughly chilled (at least 40°F).

6. Carefully strain the chilled mixture through a strainer to remove the lavender, if necessary. For a stronger flavor, using a spoon, stir in the lavender honey. Pour into an ice cream machine and churn according to the manufacturer's instructions. If making by hand, see the instructions on page 15.

7. When the churning is completed, use a spoon or spatula to scrape the ice cream into a freezer-proof container with a lid. Freeze until it reaches the correct scooping texture (at least 2 hours).

8. Decorate each portion with lavender flowers before serving.

CAN YOU LICK IT? YES, YOU CAN!

MELTS HEARTS AT 50 PACES. A LOVE LETTER TO LAVENDER SOFTLY PERFUMED WITH LEMONY OVERTONES.

Inside scoop

THE LADYCHILLER
ROSE PETAL ICE CREAM

WANT SOME HEAVY PETAL? THE DAY BEFORE WE OPENED OUR BAR IN SELREFRIGERATORS, WE WERE MAKING OUR FIRST-EVER BATCH OF ROSE PETAL ICE CREAM FOR A PHOTO SHOOT. SOMEHOW A CATFIGHT BETWEEN TWO MODELS ESCALATED INTO AN FULL-BLOWN ICE CREAM FIGHT IN LINGERIE. GIVEN THAT OUR VIRGIN BATCH OF ICE CREAM WAS BEING THROWN, CATAPULTED, AND SMEARED AROUND OUR BRAND NEW ICE CREAM BAR, I SUMMONED VAST RESERVES OF CHURCHILLIAN DETERMINATION TO SEPARATE THE TWO LADIES. AFTER SOME COVERTLY RECORDED FOOTAGE MADE IT ONTO YOUTUBE, THIS ICE CREAM BECAME AN INSTANT BEST SELLER.

• 1 cup whole milk • ½ cup heavy cream • 2 egg yolks
• ⅓ cup plus 1 tablespoon superfine or granulated sugar • 1 teaspoon vanilla extract
• ½ cup rose water • edible rose petals, to decorate

1. Pour the milk and cream into a large saucepan and heat gently, stirring occasionally, until the mixture begins to steam but not boil.

2. Meanwhile, whisk the egg yolks in a heatproof bowl until smooth. Add the sugar and salt and whisk until pale and slightly fluffy. Gradually and slowly, pour the hot milk into the egg mixture while whisking continuously to prevent the eggs from scrambling. Return the mixture to the saucepan and place over low heat, stirring frequently, until the custard thinly coats the back of a wooden spoon. Do not let boil.

3. Turn off the heat and whisk in the vanilla extract and rose water. Pour the mixture back into the bowl and set aside for about 30 minutes, stirring occasionally, until cooled to room temperature. For more rapid chilling, fill a sink halfway with cold water and ice and place the bowl of mixture in it for 20 minutes. Never put the hot mixture into the refrigerator.

4. Once cooled, cover the mixture and refrigerate, ideally overnight, but at least for 6 hours, until thoroughly chilled (at least 40°F).

5. Pour the chilled mixture into an ice cream machine and churn according to the manufacturer's instructions. If making by hand, see the instructions on page 15.

6. When the churning is completed, use a spoon or spatula to scrape the ice cream into a freezer-proof container with a lid. Freeze until it reaches the correct scooping texture (at least 2 hours).

7. Decorate each portion with edible rose petals before serving.

ANY MORE CHILLED AND SHE'LL NEED GRITTING

THE FEMME FATALE OF ICE CREAMS, ITS FRAGRANT NOTES WILL TRANSPORT YOU TO A BOUDOIR AND BEYOND

Inside scoop

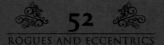
BABY GOOGOO

BREAST MILK ICE CREAM

TABOO OR NOT TABOO? THAT WAS THE QUESTION THE ICECREAMISTS POSED TO THE WORLD ON FEBRUARY 25, 2011, AS WE WERE ABOUT TO OPEN OUR FIRST PERMANENT ICE CREAM BOUTIQUE. THIS SIMPLE POLITICAL EXPERIMENT DIDN'T JUST CAUSE A RIPPLE, BUT A STORM IN A D CUP. FORMERLY KNOWN AS "BABY GAGA," BEFORE LADY GAGA PUT THE SQUEEZE ON ME. WE WANTED TO ASK WHETHER IT WAS BETTER FOR US TO CONSUME THE BODILY FLUID (BOVINE JUICE) OF ANOTHER MAMMAL, OR MOTHER'S MILK, WHICH HAS WEANED HUMANITY SAFELY FOR THOUSANDS OF YEARS WITHOUT A SINGLE RECORDED DEATH. WHY DON'T YOU SUCK IT AND SEE?

· 1 cup free-roaming, organic, and freshly squeezed breast milk
(the milk should be screened in line with medical standards for blood tests)
· ½ cup heavy cream · 2 egg yolks · ⅓ cup plus 1 tablespoon superfine or granulated sugar
· pinch of sea salt · ½ vanilla bean, split lengthwise

1. Pour the milk and cream into a large saucepan. Scrape in the vanilla seeds, then add the empty bean and heat gently, stirring occasionally, until the mixture begins to steam but not boil.

2. Meanwhile, whisk the egg yolks in a heatproof bowl until smooth. Add the sugar and salt and whisk until pale and slightly fluffy. Gradually and slowly, pour the hot milk into the egg mixture while whisking continuously to prevent the eggs from scrambling. Return the mixture to the saucepan and place over low heat, stirring frequently, until the custard thinly coats the back of a wooden spoon. Do not let boil.

3. Pour back into the bowl and set aside for about 30 minutes, stirring occasionally, until cooled to room temperature. For more rapid chilling, fill a sink halfway with cold water and ice

and place the bowl of mixture in it for 20 minutes. Never put the hot mixture into the refrigerator.

4. Once cooled, cover the mixture and refrigerate, ideally overnight, but at least for 6 hours, until thoroughly chilled (at least 40°F).

5. Remove the vanilla bean and pour the mixture into an ice cream machine. Churn according to the manufacturer's instructions. If making by hand, see the instructions on page 15.

6. When the churning is completed, use a spoon or spatula to scrape the ice cream into a freezer-proof container with a lid. Freeze until it reaches the correct scooping texture (at least 2 hours).

ABSOLUTELY DELICIOUS AND NUTRITIOUS DAVID WALLIAMS

Inside scoop BREAST MILK IS THINNER THAN COW'S MILK AND THE FLAVOR CAN VARY, DEPENDING ON WHAT THE DONOR HAS EATEN AND HOW LONG THEY HAVE BEEN BREAST-FEEDING. THE CREAM AND OTHER INGREDIENTS GIVE IT STRUCTURE AND DEPTH. IF YOU ARE COOKING FRIED PLACENTA, IT IS A GREAT DESSERT. IF NOT, MAKE IT AND MILK IT FOR ALL IT'S WORTH.

BLACK ICE
LICORICE ICE CREAM

AS ANYONE WHO KNOWS ME WILL TESTIFY, MY BODY IS A TEMPLE. A BUDDHIST TEMPLE. FRIENDS HAVE CRUELLY SUGGESTED I HAD BEEN IN TRAINING FOR THE FOLLOWING EVENTS IN THE LONDON 2012 OLYMPIC GAMES—THE DIABETICS AND THE PARALYTICS. IN RESPONSE, I THOUGHT I COULD KILL TWO BIRDS WITH ONE STONE BY UNDERGOING AN EIGHT-DAY HUNGER STRIKE OUTSIDE THE HOME OF THE PRIME MINISTER IN PROTEST ABOUT THE LACK OF EQUAL PARENTING RIGHTS IN THE UK. BY DAY 6, AN ARMED RESPONSE TEAM WERE PROTECTING DAVID CAMERON'S REFRIGERATOR AND I WOULD HAVE KILLED FOR A QUICHE. I KNEW LICORICE HAD TO BE IN THE BOOK AFTER I BEGAN HALLUCINATING ABOUT A CHARACTER MADE FROM ASSORTED LICORICE CANDIES. THE PRIME MINISTER SUBSEQUENTLY SENT ME A LETTER AS SLIPPERY AS HIS PREELECTION COMMITMENTS.

· 2½ ounces black licorice sticks, gently crushed · 1 cup whole milk · ½ cup heavy cream
· 2 egg yolks · ⅓ cup plus 1 tablespoon superfine or granulated sugar · ¼ teaspoon vanilla extract
· few drops of natural black food coloring

1. Put the licorice in a saucepan with ½ cup of water and place over low heat for 15 minutes, stirring occasionally, until the licorice has melted.

2. Meanwhile, pour the milk and cream into a large saucepan and heat gently, stirring occasionally, until the mixture begins to steam but not boil.

3. Whisk the egg yolks in a heatproof bowl until smooth. Add the sugar and vanilla and whisk until pale and slightly fluffy. Gradually and slowly, pour the hot milk into the egg mixture while whisking continuously to prevent the eggs from scrambling. Return the mixture to the saucepan, place over low heat, stir in the melted licorice, and heat until the custard thinly coats the back of a wooden spoon. Do not let boil. Add the black food coloring to desired effect.

4. Pour back into the bowl and set aside for about 30 minutes, stirring occasionally, until cooled to room temperature. For more rapid chilling, fill a sink halfway with cold water and ice and place the bowl of mixture in it for 20 minutes. Never put the hot mixture into the refrigerator.

5. Once cooled, cover the mixture and refrigerate, ideally overnight, but at least for 6 hours, until thoroughly chilled (at least 40°F). Pour the chilled mixture into an ice cream machine and churn according to the manufacturer's instructions. If making by hand, see the instructions on page 15.

6. When the churning is complete, use a spoon or spatula to scrape the ice cream into a freezer-proof container with a lid. Freeze until it reaches the correct scooping texture (at least 2 hours).

DO US A FLAVOR

Inside scoop CALABRIAN LICORICE IS PROBABLY THE BEST IN THE WORLD. THE SOIL AND CLIMATE IN CALABRIA, THE "TOE" OF ITALY, IS IDEAL FOR GROWING GLYCYRRHIZA GLABRA, THE ROOTS OF WHICH PRODUCE LICORICE WITH A BITTERSWEET TASTE THAT IS SAID TO HAVE SOOTHING PROPERTIES FOR DIGESTION AND SORE THROATS

LADY MARMALADE
SEVILLE MARMALADE ICE CREAM

MY FIRST WIFE WAS A ONE-WOMAN SPANISH INQUISITION. A LETHAL, LIBERIAN ASSASSIN WITH A STUTTERING GOOSE STEP LIKE GENERAL FRANCO IN A SKIRT. BUT IT WASN'T ALL BAD. WHEN WE WERE YOUNGER, SHE TRIED TO HAVE ME KILLED. IT WAS SEMANA SANTA (HOLY WEEK) IN SEVILLE. THE STREETS WERE OVERFLOWING WITH STREAMS OF HUMANITY POURING OUT ACROSS THE BARRIOS, AND THE AIR WAS FRAGRANT WITH ORANGE BLOSSOM. MY WIFE SUGGESTED WE VISIT THE SMALL TOWN OF ARCOS DE LA FRONTERA ON EASTER MORNING FOR A MARMALADE-ON-TOAST BREAKFAST AND AN INVIGORATING BULL RUN WITH A HALF TON OF SPANISH STEAK NUZZLING MY ASS. I NEARLY ENDED UP AS A SPANISH KEBAB THANKS TO EL TORO, BUT SURVIVED TO TELL THE TALE, UNLIKE MY TOAST.

· 1 cup whole milk · ½ cup heavy cream · 2 egg yolks
· ⅓ cup plus 1 tablespoon superfine or granulated sugar · ½ cup Seville orange marmalade,
plus extra to decorate · zest of 1 orange

1. Pour the milk and cream into a large saucepan and heat gently, stirring occasionally, until the mixture begins to steam but not boil.

2. Meanwhile, whisk the egg yolks in a heatproof bowl until smooth. Add the sugar and whisk until pale and slightly fluffy. Gradually and slowly, pour the hot milk into the egg mixture while whisking continuously to prevent the eggs from scrambling. Return the mixture to the saucepan and place over low heat, stirring frequently, until the custard thinly coats the back of a wooden spoon. Do not let boil.

3. Add the marmalade and mix with an immersion blender. Pour the mixture back into the bowl and set aside for about 30 minutes, stirring occasionally, until cooled to room temperature. For more rapid chilling, fill a sink halfway with cold water and ice and place the bowl of mixture in it for 20 minutes. Never put the hot mixture into the refrigerator.

4. Once cooled, cover the mixture and refrigerate, ideally overnight, but at least for 6 hours, until thoroughly chilled (at least 40°F). Pour the chilled mixture into an ice cream machine and churn according to the manufacturer's instructions. If making by hand, see the instructions on page 15.

5. When the churning is completed. Use a spoon or spatula to scrape the mixture into a freezer-proof container with a lid. Freeze until it reaches the correct scooping texture (at least 2 hours).

6. Decorate each portion with the orange zest and dollops of marmalade before serving.

YOU ONLY LICK TWICE

TART ANDALUSIAN ORANGE ZEST OFFSET BY A THICK, CREAMY MOUTHFEEL

Inside scoop

BORN AND BRED
SODA BREAD AND IRISH STOUT ICE CREAM

MY IRISH CLAN HAIL FROM THE VILLAGE OF SNEEM, A JEWEL ON THE RING OF KERRY. ON A ROCKY PROMONTORY STANDS PARKNASILLA HOTEL, HISTORICAL HAVEN FOR LUMINARIES SUCH AS GEORGE BERNARD SHAW, CHARLIE CHAPLIN, CHARLES DE GAULLE, AND PRINCESS GRACE OF MONACO. IT WAS THERE, IN 1977, AS A SHY, STUTTERING TEN-YEAR-OLD BOY, I MET THE THEN TAOISEACH JACK LYNCH AT THE PIER BENEATH THE HOTEL. BACK AT THE BAR. HEAD BARMAN SONNY LOONEY SERVED MY FATHER A BEAUTIFULLY POURED PINT OF GUINNESS INTO WHICH I DUNKED MY RICH, BUTTERMILK-LADEN SLICE OF SODA BREAD. MY DAD LATER TOLD ME THE O'CONNORS WERE THE LAST KINGS OF IRELAND, QUITE POSSIBLY BECAUSE WE SPENT SO MUCH TIME IN THE BAR. SLÁINTE!

• 1 cup whole milk • ½ teaspoon allspice • ½ teaspoon nutmeg • ½ cup heavy cream • 2 egg yolks
• ⅓ cup plus 1 tablespoon firmly packed brown sugar • ½ cup crumbled Irish soda bread
• ¼ cup Irish stout (such as Guinness)

FOR THE CARAMELIZED CRUMBS • ¾ cup crumbled Irish soda bread • 2 tablespoons firmly packed brown sugar

1. Pour the milk, spices, and cream into a large saucepan and heat gently, stirring occasionally, until the mixture begins to steam but not boil.

2. Meanwhile, whisk the egg yolks in a heatproof bowl until smooth. Add the sugar and whisk until slightly fluffy. Gradually and slowly, pour the hot milk into the egg mixture while whisking continuously to prevent the eggs from scrambling. Return the mixture to the saucepan and place over low heat, stirring frequently until the custard thinly coats the back of a wooden spoon. Do not let boil.

3. Add the soda bread and mix with an immersion blender, then pour the mixture back into the bowl and set aside for about 30 minutes, stirring occasionally, until cooled to room temperature. For more rapid chilling, fill a sink halfway with cold water and ice and place the bowl of mixture in it for 20 minutes. Never put the hot mixture into the refrigerator.

4. Once cooled, boil the stout until it is reduced by about half and add to the custard. Cover the mixture and refrigerate, ideally overnight, but at least for 6 hours, until thoroughly chilled (at least 40°F). Pour the chilled mixture into an ice cream machine and churn according to the manufacturer's instructions. If making by hand, see the instructions on page 15.

5. Meanwhile, prepare the topping. Combine the soda bread and sugar and spread over a shallow baking pan. Place under a medium-hot broiler, stirring frequently until the bread crumbs are softly caramelized. Let cool a little.

6. Fold all but ¼ cup of the toasted bread mixture into the ice cream, then use a spoon or spatula to scrape the ice cream into a freezer-proof container with a lid. Freeze until it reaches the correct scooping texture (at least 2 hours).

7. Decorate each portion with a few of the remaining caramelized crumbs before serving. Enjoy with a chilled pint of Irish stout.

LIKE A THICK, PILLOWY BLANKET OF CREAM, WITH A SOFT BUTTER CRUNCH OF
BREAD CRUMB AND BITTER STOUT FLAVOR

Inside scoop

FROM ROCHER WITH LOVE

PRALINE AND CHOCOLATE ICE CREAM

A GREAT PART OF IRISH LIFE IS DEATH. AFTER MY FATHER DIED, WE FLEW HIS BODY BACK TO IRELAND. A GIRL SITTING BESIDE ME ON THE PLANE ASKED IF I WAS ALONE. "NO," I SAID, "I'M WITH MY FATHER." "WHERE'S HE SITTING?" SHE ASKED. "IN THE HOLD," I SAID. "WHAT'S HE DOING IN THE HOLD?" SHE ASKED. MY IRISH RELATIVES REFUSED POINT BLACK TO BELIEVE IN HIS MORTALITY. "YOUR FATHER ALWAYS WAS A F*%&ING MAGICIAN," SAID MY UNCLE NOEL. DAD WAS FOND OF CHOCOLATE, ESPECIALLY THE GOLDEN BALLS OF FERRERO ROCHER. I HOPE HE CAN STILL TASTE THIS WHEREVER HE IS IN THE UNIVERSE.

• 1 cup whole milk • ½ cup heavy cream • 2 egg yolks • ⅓ cup plus 1 tablespoon superfine or granulated sugar • 1 cup hazelnut-chocolate spread (such as Nutella) • 6 chocolate praline balls (such as Ferrero Rocher), coarsely chopped • edible gold balls, to decorate

1. Pour the milk and cream into a large saucepan and heat gently, stirring occasionally, until the mixture begins to steam but not boil.

2. Meanwhile, whisk the egg yolks in a heatproof bowl until smooth. Add the sugar and whisk until pale and slightly fluffy. Gradually and slowly, pour the hot milk into the egg mixture while whisking continuously to prevent the eggs from scrambling. Return the mixture to the saucepan and place over low heat, stirring frequently, until the custard thinly coats the back of a wooden spoon. Do not let boil.

3. Add ⅔ cup of the hazelnut chocolate spread and mix with an immersion blender. Pour the mixture back into the bowl and set aside for about 30 minutes, stirring occasionally, until cooled to room temperature. For more rapid chilling, fill a sink halfway with cold water and ice and place the bowl of mixture in it for 20 minutes. Never put the hot mixture into the refrigerator.

4. Once cooled, cover the mixture and refrigerate, ideally overnight, but at least for 6 hours, until thoroughly chilled (at least 40°F). Pour into an ice cream machine and churn according to the manufacturer's instructions. If making by hand, see the instructions on page 15.

5. When the churning is completed, put the remaining ⅓ cup of hazelnut-chocolate spread in a heatproof bowl and microwave for 20 seconds on medium, or until runny. Fold into the ice cream along with the chocolate praline balls.

6. Use a spoon or spatula to scrape the ice cream into a freezer-proof container with a lid. Freeze until it reaches the correct scooping texture (at least 2 hours).

7. Chocoholics Anonymous can serve the ice cream with extra chocolate sauce (see page 154) and edible gold balls.

LICENSED TO CHILL

ACATHARTIC DOUBLE WHAMMY OF HAZELNUT CHOC SPREAD AND PRALINE WHIPPED TOGETHER INTO AN EXHILARATING STORM OF NUTTY COCOA FLAVORS.

Inside scoop

SMACK, CRACK, AND POP
POPCORN ICE CREAM

POPCORN HAS ALWAYS BEEN ONE OF THE HOLY GRAILS OF ICE CREAM BECAUSE OF ITS PROPENSITY TO SOFTEN. HOWEVER, IN THE SUMMER OF 2011, WE MADE A MIXTURE FOR FUN AND EVERYBODY DEVOURED IT IN SECONDS. WITH ADDICTIVE PROPERTIES LIKE THIS, WE CHRISTENED IT "SMACK, CRACK, AND POP." THIS IS AN ICE CREAM THAT'S LIKE CRACK COCAINE. IN A CONTAINER.

• 1 cup whole milk • ½ cup heavy cream • 2 egg yolks
• ⅓ cup plus 1 tablespoon superfine or granulated sugar • large pinch of sea salt
• 9 cups toffee-coated popcorn, plus extra for decorating • 1 handful mini butterscotch chips
• 1½ tablespoons Dulce de Leche Sauce, warmed (see page 154)

1. Pour the milk and cream into a large saucepan and heat gently, stirring occasionally, until the mixture begins to steam but not boil.

2. Meanwhile, whisk the egg yolks in a heatproof bowl until smooth. Add the sugar and salt and whisk until pale and slightly fluffy. Gradually and slowly, pour the hot milk into the egg mixture while whisking continuously to prevent the eggs from scrambling. Return the mixture to the saucepan and place over low heat, stirring frequently until the custard thinly coats the back of a wooden spoon. Do not let boil.

3. Add the popcorn, blend with an immersion blender, then strain the custard through a strainer. Pour back into the bowl and set aside for about 30 minutes, stirring occasionally, until cooled to room temperature. For more rapid chilling, fill a sink halfway with cold water and ice and place the bowl of mixture in it for 20 minutes. Never put the hot mixture into the refrigerator.

4. Once cooled, cover the mixture and refrigerate, ideally overnight, but at least for 6 hours, until thoroughly chilled (at least 40°F). Pour the chilled mixture into an ice cream machine and churn according to the manufacturer's instructions. If making by hand, see the instructions on page 15.

5. When the churning is completed, fold a handful (or as many as you want) of the butterscotch chips into the ice cream. Use a spoon or spatula to scrape it into a freezer-proof container with a lid. Freeze until it reaches the correct scooping texture (at least 2 hours).

6. Drizzle each portion with a little warmed sauce and decorate with the extra popcorn before serving.

GIMME SOME SUGAR, BABY BRUCE CAMPBELL, ARMY OF DARKNESS

HIGHLY ADDICTIVE CHEWY CARAMEL NOTES FOLLOWED BY CRUNCHY BUTTERSCOTCH PIECES AND POPCORN BITES. THIS IS POP-TRASH ICE CREAM AT ITS FINEST.

Inside scoop

THE MICHELIN MAN
MARSHMALLOW ICE CREAM

AT THE ICECREAMISTS WE SAY, "MARSHMALLOW MAKETH THE MAN." AS SOMEONE WHO HAS OCCASIONAL BOUTS OF WARDROBE DYSFUNCTION, I CAN REGULARLY BE SEEN ON GOOGLE EARTH WEARING SOME COLORFUL GARMENTS THAT ACCOMODATE A MAN WHOSE SIZE REFLECTS HIS DEDICATION TO HIS ART. IN A PREVIOUS LIFE, I WAS AFFLICTED BY A FASCINATION FOR LYCRA SUPERSUITS, BROUGHT TO NATIONAL ATTENTION DURING MY CAMPAIGNING DAYS. FEW PEOPLE WILL SYMPATHIZE WITH THE PITFALLS OF WEARING TIGHT, STRETCHY POLYESTER GARMENTS AND SUPERHERO GARB, BUT THE CHANCES ARE THAT YOU WILL LOOK MORE LIKE THE MICHELIN MAN THAN SUPERMAN, WITH PILLOWY EXPANSES OF MARSHMALLOW EXPANDING INTO PLACES WHERE NO LYCRA HAS EVER GONE BEFORE.

• 1 cup whole milk • ½ cup heavy cream • 2 egg yolks
• ⅓ cup plus 1 tablespoon superfine or granulated sugar • 16 large marshmallows
• a few miniature marshmallows, to decorate

FOR THE RIPPLE • 1 cup miniature mixed marshmallows
• 1 cup Marshmallow Fluff (crème)

1. Pour the milk and cream into a large saucepan and heat gently, stirring occasionally, until the mixture begins to steam but not boil.

2. Meanwhile, whisk the egg yolks in a heatproof bowl until smooth. Add the sugar and whisk until pale and slightly fluffy. Gradually and slowly, pour the hot milk into the egg mixture while whisking continuously to prevent the eggs from scrambling. Return the mixture to the saucepan and place over low heat, stirring frequently, until the custard thinly coats the back of a wooden spoon. Do not let boil.

3. Stir the large marshmallows into the warm custard until melted. Pour back into the bowl and set aside for about 30 minutes, stirring occasionally, until cooled to room temperature. For more rapid chilling, fill a sink halfway with cold water and ice and place the bowl of mixture in it for 20 minutes. Never put the hot mixture into the refrigerator.

4. Once cooled, cover the mixture and refrigerate, ideally overnight, but at least for 6 hours, until thoroughly chilled (at least 40°F). Pour the chilled mixture into an ice cream machine and churn according to the manufacturer's instructions. If making by hand, see the instructions on page 15.

5. When the churning is completed, fold in the miniature marshmallows and marshmallow crème. Use a spoon or spatula to scrape the ice cream into a freezer-proof container with a lid. Freeze until it reaches the correct scooping texture (at least 2 hours).

6. Decorate each portion with a few miniature marshmallows before serving.

RELEASE YOUR INNER CHILD WITH THIS FLUFFY REMAKE OF THE OLD TUCK SHOP FAVORITE

Inside scoop

THE CAKED CRUSADER
JAMAICAN GINGER CAKE ICE CREAM

MY LATE BUSINESS PARTNER, PETER MATTHEWS, WAS AN ENTREPRENEUR WITH A SCHOOLBOYISH WIT AND EXTRAORDINARY ENERGY. PETER MATTHEWS' PARTIES WERE THE STUFF OF LEGEND, AND HE WAS FOREVER GETTING EMBROILED IN NEAR-DEATH YET LIFE-AFFIRMING EXPERIENCES THAT ENCOURAGED HIM TO PURSUE EVER MORE RECKLESS BEHAVIOR. WHEN HE WAS REPORTED DEAD IN AN ACCIDENT ABROAD, ONE COULDN'T HELP THINK HE HAD FAKED HIS OWN DEMISE IN AN ATTEMPT TO EVADE THE TAX INSPECTOR. I IMAGINE HE IS NOW RESIDING UNDER A VARIETY OF NOMS DE PLUME. BEING A GINGER, AS WE CALL REDHEADS IN THE UK, HE WAS PARTIAL TO THIS CAKE, SO THIS ONE IS FOR PETER, WHEREVER YOU ARE …

· 1 cup whole milk · ½ cup heavy cream · 2 egg yolks · ⅓ cup plus 1 tablespoon superfine or granulated sugar
· 1 heaping teaspoon ground ginger, plus extra for dusting · 1 store-bought ginger cake
· 2 balls of perserved ginger, chopped · slug of preserved ginger syrup · dark rum, to serve (optional)
FOR THE SUGAR SYRUP · ⅓ cup superfine or granulated sugar · ⅓ cup water

1. Pour the milk and cream into a large saucepan and heat gently, stirring occasionally, until the mixture begins to steam but not boil.

2. Meanwhile, whisk the egg yolks in a heatproof bowl until smooth. Add the superfine sugar and whisk until pale and slightly fluffy. Gradually and slowly, pour the hot milk into the egg mixture while whisking continuously to prevent the eggs from scrambling. Return the mixture to the saucepan, add the ground ginger, and place over low heat, stirring frequently until the custard thinly coats the back of a wooden spoon. Do not let boil.

3. Pour back into the bowl and set aside for about 30 minutes, stirring occasionally, until cooled to room temperature. For more rapid chilling, fill a sink halfway with cold water and ice and place the bowl of mixture in it for 20 minutes. Never put the hot mixture into the refrigerator.

4. When chilled, add about 3 ounces of the cake, the preserved ginger and syrup, and blend until smooth. Cover and refrigerate, ideally overnight, but at least for 6 hours, until thoroughly chilled (at least 40°F). Pour the chilled mixture into an ice cream machine and churn according to the manufacturer's instructions. If making by hand, see the instructions on page 15.

5. When the churning is completed, prepare the sugar syrup by putting the sugar and water in a saucepan over medium heat and stirring until the sugar dissolves. Let simmer for a few minutes, until the liquid becomes a syrup.

6. Thinly slice the remaining cake and drizzle the sugar syrup over it until damp but not saturated. Fold the cake through the ice cream, then scrape into a freezer-proof container with a lid. Freeze until it reaches the correct scooping texture (at least 2 hours). For an extra kick, dust each portion with a little more ground ginger, or add a slug of dark rum before serving.

COOLING CREAM RIPPLED WITH RICH, MOIST CAKE AND A PENETRATING KICK LIKE A GINGER JAVELIN

Inside scoop

THE BAILOUT

IRISH CREAM LIQUEUR AND BRANDY ICE CREAM

JULIE WAS THE BEWITCHING IRISH TEMPTRESS AT THE HORSESHOE BAR OF THE SHELBOURNE HOTEL IN DUBLIN, IRELAND, WHO INTRODUCED ME TO THIS MILITARILY UPGRADED VERSION OF BAILEYS, FUEL-INJECTED WITH A DOUBLE SHOT OF BRANDY. IN 2005, WHEN MRS. O' AND I ENJOYED A FILTHY WEEKEND IN THE ENGLISH SEASIDE TOWN OF BRIGHTON, THE AFTERNOON WAS LOST CONSUMING DOUBLE BAILEYS AND BRANDY. BRIGHTON CERTAINLY ROCKED BECAUSE NINE MONTHS LATER WE HAD ANOTHER SOUVENIR TO GO WITH THE SOUVENIR HAT AND STICK OF CANDY—OUR SON ARCHIE.

· 1 cup whole milk · ½ cup heavy cream · 2 egg yolks · ⅓ cup plus 1 tablespoon superfine or granulated sugar · ¼ cup Irish Cream liqueur (such as Baileys), plus extra to serve · 2 teaspoons brandy

1. Pour the milk and cream into a large saucepan and heat gently, stirring occasionally, until the mixture begins to steam but not boil.

2. Meanwhile, whisk the egg yolks in a heatproof bowl until smooth. Add the sugar and whisk until pale and slightly fluffy. Gradually and slowly, pour the hot milk into the egg mixture while whisking continuously to prevent the eggs from scrambling. Return the mixture to the saucepan and place over low heat, stirring frequently, until the custard thinly coats the back of a wooden spoon. Do not let boil.

3. Stir in the Irish cream liqueur and brandy, then pour the mixture back into the bowl and set aside for about 30 minutes, stirring occasionally, until cooled to room temperature. For more rapid chilling, fill a sink halfway with cold water and ice and place the bowl of mixture in it for 20 minutes. Never put the hot mixture into the refrigerator.

4. Once cooled, cover the mixture and refrigerate, ideally overnight, but at least for 6 hours, until thoroughly chilled (at least 40°F). Pour the chilled mixture into an ice cream machine and churn according to the manufacturer's instructions. If making by hand, see the instructions on page 15.

5. When the churning is completed, use a spoon or spatula to scrape the ice cream into a freezer-proof container with a lid. Freeze until it reaches the correct scooping texture (at least 2 hours).

6. Pour a little extra Baileys on each portion before serving.

YOU CAN ENJOY ICECREAMISM ANYWHERE: AGAINST THE BAR, AGAINST THE WALL, AND AGAINST THE LAW

LIKE A BREATHLESS IRISH BANSHEE—DECADENT AND CREAMY WITH AN UNEXPECTED CELTIC KICK

DOUGHNUT STOP BELIEVIN'

JELLY DOUGHNUT ICE CREAM

WHY IS IT THAT AS SOON AS THE GOVERNMENT SEES US ENJOYING SOMETHING THEY WANT TO TAX IT? WHEN WE HEARD ABOUT THE "FAT TAX" IN THE UK, WE WENT WHERE NO RESPONSIBLE ICE CREAM MAN HAD GONE BEFORE AND CAME UP WITH THE IDEA OF THE "DOH-LYMPICS." SCOFF YOUR WAY THROUGH 5 DOUGHNUT RINGS AND 2,012 CALORIES PER PORTION OF THE WORLD'S FATTEST ICE CREAM. OUR OLYMPIC MOTTO "SLOWER, LOWER, FATTER."

• 1 cup whole milk • 1 teaspoon ground cinnamon • ½ cup heavy cream • 2 egg yolks • ⅓ cup plus 1 tablespoon superfine or granulated sugar • 2 plain ring doughnuts • a few fresh raspberries, to decorate

FOR THE RIPPLE • ¼ cup raspberry jelly • ¼ cup fresh raspberries • ⅓ cup superfine or granulated sugar • ⅓ cup water • 2 ring doughnuts, chopped into bite-size pieces

1. Pour the milk, cinnamon, and cream into a large saucepan and heat gently, stirring occasionally, until the mixture begins to steam but not boil.

2. Meanwhile, whisk the egg yolks in a heatproof bowl until smooth. Add the sugar and whisk until pale and slightly fluffy. Gradually and slowly, pour the hot milk into the egg mixture while whisking continuously to prevent the eggs from scrambling. Return the mixture to the saucepan and place over low heat, stirring frequently, until the custard thinly coats the back of a wooden spoon. Do not let boil.

3. Blend the doughnuts into the warm custard using an immersion blender until the mixture is smooth. Pour back into the bowl and set aside for about 30 minutes, stirring occasionally, until cooled to room temperature. For more rapid chilling, fill a sink halfway with cold water and ice and place the bowl of mixture in it for 20 minutes. Never put the hot mixture into the refrigerator.

4. Once cooled, cover the mixture and refrigerate, ideally overnight, but at least for 6 hours, until thoroughly chilled (at least 40°F). Pour the chilled mixture into an ice cream machine and churn according to the manufacturer's instructions. If making by hand, see the instructions on page 15.

5. When the churning is completed, prepare the ripple by mashing the jelly and raspberries together with a fork. Set aside.

6. Place the sugar and water in a saucepan over medium heat and stir until the sugar dissolves. Let simmer for a few minutes, until the liquid becomes a syrup. Put the doughnut pieces into the syrup until lightly soaked, but not saturated or falling apart. Fold into the ice cream along with the raspberry mixture. Use a spoon or spatula to scrape the ice cream into a freezer-proof container with a lid. Freeze until it reaches the correct scooping texture (at least 2 hours).

7. Decorate each portion with few raspberries before serving.

Inside scoop THIS IS AN ICE CREAM THAT IS FULL OF FAT AND GETTING FATTER. TO CUT THROUGH THE ARTERY-CLOGGING CALORIES, IT'S RIPPLED WITH JELLY AND FRESH, TART RASPBERRIES, WHICH WILL DELAY THE ONSET OF A CORONARY LONG ENOUGH FOR YOU TO SINK A FEW EXTRA SCOOPS

COMPLETELY PEANUTS

PEANUT BUTTER ICE CREAM

I ALWAYS WONDERED WHY REHAB WAS SO EXPENSIVE—YOU WENT IN WITH ONE ADDICTION AND LEFT WITH FOUR. AFTER GROUP SEX, ALCOHOL SMUGGLING, AND GAMBLING ADDICTION, PEANUT BUTTER SANDWICHES CAME AS SOMETHING OF AN ANTICLIMAX. I WASN'T A HUGE FAN, BUT IN REHAB IT WAS THE DRUG DU JOUR—ON TOAST. AFTER MY SECOND SLICE, I UNDERWENT A DAMASCENE CONVERSION AND BECAME A BORN-AGAIN PEANUT BUTTER BELIEVER. DURING MY SUBSEQUENT "SHARE," I TOLD THEM THAT REHAB WAS FOR QUITTERS AND MY HIGHER POWER HAD REVEALED ITSELF IN THE SHAPE OF PEANUT BUTTER ICE CREAM.

• 1 cup whole milk • ½ cup heavy cream • 2 egg yolks • ⅓ cup plus 1 tablespoon superfine or granulated sugar • large pinch of sea salt • 1 cup peanut butter • 3 tablespoons chopped unsalted peanuts, plus a few extra to decorate • brioche slices

1. Pour the milk and cream into a large saucepan and heat gently, stirring occasionally, until the mixture begins to steam but not boil.

2. Meanwhile, whisk the egg yolks in a heatproof bowl until smooth. Add the sugar and whisk until pale and slightly fluffy. Gradually and slowly, pour the hot milk into the egg mixture while whisking continuously to prevent the eggs from scrambling. Return the mixture to the saucepan and place over low heat, stirring frequently, until the custard thinly coats the back of a wooden spoon. Do not let boil.

3. Pour back into the bowl and set aside for about 30 minutes, stirring occasionally, until cooled to room temperature. For more rapid chilling, fill a sink halfway with cold water and ice and place the bowl of mixture in it for 20 minutes. Never put the hot mixture into the refrigerator.

4. Once cooled, cover the mixture and refrigerate, ideally overnight, but at least for 6 hours, until thoroughly chilled (at least 40°F).

5. Blend in ⅔ cup of the peanut butter using an immersion blender, then pour the mixture into an ice cream machine and churn according to manufacturer's instructions. If making by hand, see the instructions on page 15.

6. When the churning is completed, put the remaining peanut butter into a heatproof dish and microwave on medium in 20-second bursts until warm but not hot. Fold into the ice cream along with the chopped peanuts. Use a spoon or spatula to scrape the ice cream into a freezer-proof container with a lid. Freeze until it reaches the correct scooping texture (at least 2 hours).

7. Decorate each serving with a few peanuts processed in a blender and serve on toasted brioche slices.

MIND YOUR INNER CHILD

COLD SWEAT

CHILE, GINGER, AND LEMONGRASS ICE CREAM

MELT INTO THE PARADOX OF THE HOTTEST ICE CREAM ON EARTH. A SELF-IMMOLATING FIREBALL OF MIXED CHILES, FRESH GINGER, AND LEMONGRASS HOT LICKS, OFFSET WITH THE COOLING POWER OF FRESHLY MADE GELATO. WHEN LIT, STAND WELL BACK AND BE SURE ALL WOMEN, CHILDREN, AND PETS ARE KEPT INSIDE.

• 1 cup whole milk • ½ cup heavy cream • 2 egg yolks • ⅓ cup plus 1 tablespoon superfine or granulated sugar • pinch of sea salt • 1 red chile, seeded and finely chopped • thumb-size piece of fresh ginger, peeled and coarsely grated • 1 stick of lemongrass, finely chopped • chili oil, to serve

1. Pour the milk and cream into a large saucepan and heat gently, stirring occasionally, until the mixture begins to steam but not boil.

2. Meanwhile, whisk the egg yolks in a heatproof bowl until smooth. Add the sugar and whisk until pale and slightly fluffy. Gradually and slowly, pour the hot milk into the egg mixture while whisking continuously to prevent the eggs from scrambling. Return the mixture to the saucepan and place over low heat, stirring frequently, until the custard thinly coats the back of a wooden spoon. Do not let boil.

3. Add the chile, ginger, and lemongrass to the custard and blend until smooth. Strain twice through a strainer or cheesecloth to remove all fibers and seeds. Pour back into the bowl and set aside for about 30 minutes, stirring occasionally, until cooled to room temperature. For more rapid chilling, fill a sink halfway with cold water and ice and place the bowl of mixture in it for 20 minutes. Never put the hot mixture into the refrigerator.

4. Once cooled, cover the mixture and refrigerate, ideally overnight, but at least for 6 hours, until thoroughly chilled (at least 40°F). Pour the chilled mixture into an ice cream machine and churn according to the manufacturer's instructions. If making by hand, see the instructions on page 15.

5. When the churning is completed, use a spoon or spatula to scrape the ice cream into a freezer-proof container with a lid. Freeze until it reaches the correct scooping texture (at least 2 hours). Serve in cones.

6. Drizzle each portion with chili oil before serving.

EMERGENCY COLD RELIEF

Inside scoop THIS IS A MASOCHISTIC TRIPLE WHAMMY OF SWEET, SAVORY, AND SPICY FLAVORS. AN ICE CREAM THAT WILL BOMB, BURN, AND FLAME YOUR MOUTH INTO SUBMISSION BEFORE TASERING YOU INTO BLISSFUL PARALYSIS. UPGRADE YOUR SPRINKLER SYSTEM BEFORE CONSUMING.

RUMBLE IN THE JUNGLE

HOT BUTTERED RUM AND RAISIN ICE CREAM

THIS IS A RECIPE THAT FLOATS LIKE A BUTTERFLY AND STINGS LIKE A BEE, TO PARAPHRASE THE LEGENDARY BOXER MUHAMMAD ALI HIMSELF. "YOUR LIPS CAN'T LICK WHAT YOUR EYES CAN'T SEE." IN ANYONE'S LANGUAGE, IT'S A KNOCKOUT. OUR ROCKET-FUELED VERSION OF A TRADITIONAL RUM AND RAISIN ICE CREAM CONTAINS RUM-LACED RAISINS THAT DELIVER A DISORIENTATING RIGHT-HAND LEAD PUNCH FOLLOWED BY A COUPLE OF SHARP, JUICY JABS. IT HAS AN EXTRA ZAP OF SAILOR JERRY SPICED RUM, BEFORE BEING COUNTED OUT WITH A HOT BUTTERED RUM SAUCE.

⅓ cup raisins · 2 slugs of Sailor Jerry Spiced Rum, or similar good-quality rum
1 cup whole milk · ½ cup heavy cream · ½ vanilla bean, split lengthwise
2 egg yolks · ⅓ cup plus 1 tablespoon firmly packed brown sugar

FOR THE HOT BUTTERED RUM SAUCE · 6 tablespoons unsalted butter · ¼ cup firmly packed brown sugar
¼ cup heavy cream · 1 tablespoon corn syrup · slug of Sailor Jerry Spiced Rum, or similar good-quality rum

1. Soak the raisins in a slug of rum overnight, or for a minimum of 6 hours.

2. Pour the milk and cream into a large saucepan, scrape in the vanilla seeds, then add the empty bean and heat gently, stirring occasionally, until the mixture begins to steam but not boil.

3. Meanwhile, whisk the egg yolks in a heatproof bowl until smooth. Add the sugar and whisk until slightly fluffy. Gradually and slowly pour the hot milk into the egg mixture while whisking continuously to prevent the eggs from scrambling. Return the mixture to the saucepan and place over low heat, stirring frequently, until the custard thinly coats the back of a wooden spoon. Do not let boil.

4. Pour back into the bowl and set aside for about 30 minutes, stirring occasionally until cooled to room temperature. For more rapid chilling, fill a sink halfway with cold water and ice and place the bowl of mixture in it for 20 minutes. Never put the hot mixture into the refrigerator.

5. Once the custard is chilled, remove the vanilla bean, then stir in the raisins and their soaking liquids and add an extra slug of rum for good measure. Pour into an ice cream machine and churn according to manufacturer's instructions. If making by hand, see the instructions on page 15.

6. When the churning is completed, use a spoon or spatula to scrape the ice cream into a freezer-proof container with a lid. Freeze until it reaches the correct scooping texture (at least 2 hours).

7. To make the sauce, melt the butter in a saucepan over medium heat. Add the sugar, cream, and corn syrup and mix until the sugar has dissolved. Simmer until the sauce has thickened, then remove from heat and stir in a slug of rum. Pour some of the hot sauce over each serving of ice cream.

"A SWAGGERING REINVENTION OF A CLASSIC FOR DIE-HARD SEA SALTS, WHICH PUNCHES ABOVE ITS WEIGHT. AN EXTRA LICK OF SPICED RUM GIVES THIS ICE CREAM ITS 'RAISIN D'ÊTRE.'"

Inside scoop

SEX BOMB
STIMULANT ICE CREAM

THE ICE CREAM THE AUTHORITIES COULDN'T DEFUSE. ORIGINALLY CALLED THE SEX PISTOL DURING OUR TWO-MONTH GUERRILLA ICE CREAM POP-UP IN SELREFRIGERATORS IN 2009, THIS WAS THE FIRST OF OUR SHOCK 'N' ROLL ICE CREAMS. LACED WITH ENOUGH ERECTILE PROPERTIES TO BRING PEOPLE BACK FROM THE DEAD, IT INCURRED THE WRATH OF JOHNNY ROTTEN, THE SEX PISTOLS, LIVE NATION, AND A PHARMA GIANT. ON THE STRENGTH OF THIS, THE PROPRIETOR OF SELREFRIGERATORS, GALEN WESTON, FLEW IN FROM CANADA TO TRY THE MEDICATION FOR HIMSELF.

· 1 cup whole milk · ½ cup heavy cream · 2 egg yolks
· ⅓ cup plus 1 tablespoon superfine or granulated sugar · 3 drops each of ginkgo biloba,
arginine, and guarana · juice of 1 lemon · grated zest of ½ a lemon, plus extra to decorate

1. Pour the milk and cream into a large saucepan and heat gently, stirring occasionally, until the mixture begins to steam but not boil.

2. Meanwhile, whisk the egg yolks in a heatproof bowl until smooth. Add the sugar and whisk until pale and slightly fluffy. Gradually and slowly, pour the hot milk into the egg mixture while whisking continuously to prevent the eggs from scrambling. Return the mixture to the saucepan and place over low heat, stirring frequently, until the custard thinly coats the back of a wooden spoon. Do not let boil.

3. Pour back into the bowl and set aside for about 30 minutes, stirring occasionally, until cooled to room temperature. For more rapid chilling, fill a sink halfway with cold water and ice and place the bowl of mixture in it for 20 minutes. Never put the hot mixture into the refrigerator. Once cooled, cover the mixture and refrigerate, ideally overnight, but at least for 6 hours, until thoroughly chilled (at least 40°F).

4. Add the ginkgo, arginine, guarana, lemon juice, and zest to the chilled mixture and whisk well. Pour into an ice cream machine and churn according to the manufacturer's instructions. If making by hand, see the instructions on page 15.

5. When the churning is completed, use a spoon or spatula to scrape the ice cream into a freezer-proof container with a lid. Freeze until it reaches the correct scooping texture (at least 2 hours).

6. Decorate each portion with little extra lemon zest before serving.

BUY THE TICKET, TAKE THE RIDE HUNTER S. THOMPSON

CLASSIC ITALIAN FIOR DI LATTE ICE CREAM WITH A GENTLE LEMON SYLLABUB AND CITRUS ZEST INFUSION. LACED WITH NATURAL STIMULANTS FOR ENHANCED PERFORMANCE.

USED IN ≫

THE
ABOMINABULL
SNOWMAN

PAGE 130

ALEXANDER McCREAM
SPICED PUMPKIN ICE CREAM

FOR HALLOWEEN, WE ATTEMPTED TO BREAK THE RECORD FOR THE WORLD'S LOUDEST SCREAM—THE ACKNOWLEDGED "SCREAM OF ICE CREAM." TO COINCIDE WITH THE ATTEMPT WE CREATED THE WORLD'S FIRST "ICE CREAM SOUP," A BOWL OF STEAMING HOT PUMPKIN SOUP WITH A SCOOP OF PUMPKIN ICE CREAM DROPPED IN THE MIDDLE. I LOVED IT, BUT IT LEFT EVERYONE ELSE IN MELTDOWN. IN THE END WE RAN OUT OF TIME TO STAGE THE WORLD-RECORD ATTEMPT, AND KILLED OFF ICE CREAM SOUP, BUT WE KEPT SPICED PUMPKIN ICE CREAM ALIVE.

- 1 cup whole milk · ½ cup heavy cream · 2 egg yolks
- ½ cup plus 1 tablespoon superfine or granulated sugar · ⅓ cup canned pumpkin
- ½ teaspoon ground cinnamon, plus extra for dusting · drop of vanilla extract
- dash of dark rum (optional)

1. Pour the milk and cream into a large saucepan and heat gently, stirring occasionally, until the mixture begins to steam but not boil.

2. Meanwhile, whisk the egg yolks in a heatproof bowl until smooth. Add ⅓ cup of the sugar and whisk until pale and slightly fluffy. Gradually and slowly, pour the hot milk into the egg mixture while whisking continuously to prevent the eggs from scrambling. Return the mixture to the saucepan and place over low heat, stirring frequently, until the custard thinly coats the back of a wooden spoon. Do not let boil.

3. Pour back into the bowl and set aside for about 30 minutes, stirring occasionally, until cooled to room temperature. For more rapid chilling, fill a sink halfway with cold water and ice and place the bowl of mixture in it for 20 minutes. Never put the hot mixture into the refrigerator.

4. Put the pumpkin, cinnamon, vanilla extract, remaining sugar, and a dash of rum, if using, into a blender or food processor and blend until smooth. Add to the chilled custard and whisk well. Pour the mixture into an ice cream machine and churn according to the manufacturer's instructions. If making by hand, see the instructions on page 15.

5. When the churning is completed, use a spoon or spatula to scrape the ice cream into a freezer-proof container with a lid. Freeze until it reaches the correct scooping texture (at least 2 hours). Dust each portion with a little ground cinnamon before serving.

THE DEVIL HAS ALL THE BEST LICKS

TAKE A TRIP TO THE DARK SIDE WITH THIS CUT-THROAT LICK OF AUTUMNAL FLAVORS

Inside scoop

THE SAVOY CHILL
EARL GREY SORBETTO

THE MEETING AT THE SAVOY HOTEL WAS A BLEND OF DISTINCTIVE FLAVORS AND THE SCENT OF A WOMAN WHO INDUCED MORE THAN A LITTLE "HOO-HA." I SAT LIKE A DISOBEDIENT SCHOOLBOY IN THE PRESENCE OF A "GOLD COMMANDER" FROM SCOTLAND YARD. HER MISSION WAS TO PRY OUT OF ME ANY FUTURE PLANS FOR GLOBAL DOMINATION. I PLEADED MY INNOCENCE AND TOLD HER I WAS IN THE MIDDLE OF WRITING A BOOK ON THE ICECREAMISTS. TO THIS DAY, I CANNOT FIGURE OUT WHY A SENIOR OFFICER INTERROGATING AN ICE CREAM MAN WAS DRESSED LIKE A KISSOGRAM IN A COCKTAIL DRESS AND FISHNET STOCKINGS AT 10:00 IN THE MORNING IN THE SAVOY HOTEL. BEING GRATEFUL SHE DIDN'T ASK IF IT WAS A POLICEMAN'S CLUB IN MY POCKET, OR IF I WAS JUST PLEASED TO SEE HER, I MADE MY EXCUSES AND DEPARTED, BUT NOT UNTIL I HAD DRANK THE LAST OF MY EARL GREY TEA AND GIVEN HER A WICKED WINK. WHEN I RETIRED TO THE SANCTUARY OF THE ICECREAMISTS, THEY MADE ME THIS CALMING "EARLY GREY" SORBETTO IN HONOR OF THE LADY FROM THE YARD.

- 2 cups boiling water · ⅔ cup superfine or granulated sugar· 2 Earl Grey tea bags
- zest and juice of 1 lemon · ½ an egg white

1. Pour the water and sugar into a bowl, add the tea bags, and stir together. Let steep for 10 minutes, then add the lemon juice and stir again. Cover and refrigerate, ideally overnight, until thoroughly chilled (at least 40°F).

2. Remove tea bags and pour into an ice cream machine. Churn according to the manufacturer's instructions. If making by hand, see the instructions on page 15. Halfway through, add the egg white.

3. When the churning is completed, use a spoon or spatula to scrape the sorbetto into a freezer-proof container with a lid. Freeze until it reaches the correct scooping texture (at least 2–3 hours).

4. Decorate each portion with a little lemon zest before serving.

THE WHIRL IS NOT ENOUGH

Inside scoop A METROPOLITAN BLEND OF LIGHT AND DISTINCTIVE BERGAMOT FLAVOR WITH CITRUS NOTES—PURE GOLD. FOR A "CHILLY BILLY" SORBETTO, USE LADY GREY TEA BAGS INSTEAD. THESE IMPART THE FLAVOR OF BERGAMOT WITH HINTS OF ORANGE AND LEMON.

ANY PORT IN A STORM

MULLED WINE AND PORT SORBETTO

COME ALL YE UNFAITHFUL FOR A SEASONAL SORBETTO THAT'S DANGEROUS AT BOTH ENDS AND FRISKY IN THE MIDDLE. THIS LITTLE ELF HAZARD CAME AROUND WHEN WE WERE SCREAMING FOR A BLACK CHRISTMAS WHILE TRYING TO RECRUIT AN ELITE TEAM OF LOLLIPOP-LICKING BLACK DWARVES. APPARENTLY, THERE IS A SHORTAGE OF BLACK DWARVES. WHICH SOUNDS LIKE A TALL STORY INVOLVING SOME SMALL TALK. BUT IN THE END WE WENT WITH PLAN B—A MULLED WINE AND PORT SORBETTO WITH ENOUGH PULLING POWER TO KEEP YOU BUSY UNDER THE MISTLETOE WHILE SOMEBODY PULLS YOUR CRACKER.

· ½ cup water · ½ cup superfine or granulated sugar · ⅔ cup red wine
· 1 tablespoon ground allspice · zap of ground cinnamon and nutmeg
· juice of 1 lemon, plus 1 teaspoon zest · juice of 1 orange · slug of port

TO SERVE · cinnamon sticks · orange slices

1. Pour the water into a saucepan and add the sugar. Place over low heat and bring to a boil, whisking often, until the sugar dissolves. Reduce the heat and let simmer for 5 minutes, continuing to whisk until the liquid turns into a syrup.

2. Pour the syrup into a heatproof bowl and set aside for about 30 minutes, stirring occasionally, until cooled to room temperature. For more rapid chilling, fill a sink halfway with cold water and ice and place the bowl of mixture in it for 20 minutes.

3. Heat the wine, spices, lemon juice and orange juice in a saucepan and simmer for 5 minutes. Let cool for 10 minutes, then add a slug of port. Pour into a bowl, cover, and refrigerate, ideally overnight, until thoroughly chilled (at least 40°F).

4. Pour the chilled mixture into an ice cream machine and churn according to the manufacturer's instructions. If making by hand, see the instructions on page 15.

5. When the churning is completed, use a spoon or spatula to scrape the sorbetto into a freezer-proof container with a lid. Freeze until it reaches the correct scooping texture (at least 2–3 hours).

6. Add a cinnamon stick and orange slice to each portion before serving.

FEAR NOT. IF YOUR SPRAY TAN IS FADING, PEC IMPLANTS HAVE LEAKED, AND YOUR HALOGEN TEETH HAVE FALLEN OUT, OUR WINTER WHIPLASH IS PUMPED FULL OF ENOUGH FESTIVE FLAVOR AND WINTER SPICES TO PRESERVE YOU FOR AT LEAST ANOTHER 12 MONTHS

Inside scoop

2 scoops of Sex Bomb ice cream

1 shot of ice-cold absinthe (80 percent proof minimum)

SERVES: 1 **PREPARATION:** 5 minutes when the ice cream is already prepared

Sex Bomb

A PHARMACEUTICAL GIANT BLACKLISTED IT. THE SEX PISTOLS TRIED TO BAN IT, AND THE MEXICAN AUTHORITIES IMPOUNDED IT. BOOK YOUR SEAT IN THE BLAST ZONE WITH THE ONE ICE CREAM THE AUTHORITIES COULDN'T DEFUSE, OUR INFAMOUS SEX BOMB ICE CREAM COCKTAIL. THIS ROCKET-PROPELLED ICE CREAM IS LACED WITH NATURAL STIMULANTS (GINKGO BILOBA, ARGININE, AND GUARANA) FOR A CARDIOVASCULAR WORKOUT, OFFSET WITH A MEDICINAL TWIST OF CITRUS ZEST. TOPPED WITH A SHOT OF BURNING ABSINTHE ADMINISTERED STRAIGHT FROM THE BOTTLE FOR EXPLOSIVE RESULTS.

1 Place the ice cream in a martini glass.

2 Freeze the absinthe for at least an hour before serving. Pour the absinthe into a shot glass, set alight, and pour over ice cream.

Inside scoop AN INNOCENT CREAMY MOUTHFEEL WITH A DECEPTIVELY INNOCENT CITRUS INFUSION, FOLLOWED BY AN IMMOBILIZING SHOT OF ABSINTHE THAT'S LIKE BEING HIT IN THE FACE BY A TRANQUILIZER DART

USES »

SEX BOMB
ICE CREAM

PAGE 75

Tabasco sauce	chili oil
dried red pepper flakes	1 shot of chilled chili vodka (see below)
2 scoops of Cold Sweat ice cream	SERVES: 1 PREPARATION: 10 minutes when the ice cream is already prepared
1 fresh red chile, seeded and finely chopped	
1 teaspoon finely chopped preserved ginger	

Apocalypse Chow

IF YOU LOVE THE SMELL OF GINGER IN THE MORNING, MELT INTO THIS PARADOX— THE HOTTEST ICE CREAM ON EARTH. MORE INCENDIARY THAN AN AFGHAN FUEL DEPOT, MESSIER THAN A BP OIL SPILL, A FIREBOMB OF CHILES, GINGER, AND TABASCO SERVED IN A MARTINI GLASS NAPALM-RIMMED WITH TABASCO AND DRIED RED PEPPER FLAKES. FINISHED WITH A SELF-IMMOLATING SHOT OF FLAMING CHILI VODKA, THIS IS THE ULTIMATE "SLASH 'N' BURN" ICE CREAM APOCALYPSE GUARANTEED TO PUT HAIRS ON YOUR CHEST—THEN SINGE THEM. BRRRR ...

1 Take 2 saucers and drizzle one with Tabasco, the other in red pepper flakes. Dip the rim of a martini glass first in the Tabasco, then in the pepper flakes.

2 Place the ice cream in the glass. Decorate with the chopped chile and ginger, and sprinkle with chili oil. Serve with a shot of chili vodka poured over the top and set alight.

Inside scoop

A SCORCHED-EARTH INFUSION OF EASTERN HEAT, OFFSET WITH SOOTHING ICE CREAM. TO MAKE YOUR OWN CHILI VODKA, FILL A BOTTLE OF 80 PERCENT VODKA WITH WHOLE RED CHILES AND LET MARINATE FOR A FEW DAYS

USES ≫

COLD SWEAT
ICE CREAM

PAGE 73

2 scoops of Vanilla Monologues ice cream

· 2 tablespoons ice-cold Limoncello

¼ cup chilled prosecco

2 teaspoons freshly squeezed lemon juice

SERVES: 1 PREPARATION: 10 minutes when the ice cream is already prepared

The Crybaby

HERE'S OUR SURROGATE ALCOHOLIC INTERPRETATION OF THE STORM IN A D CUP THAT WAS BABY GAGA. A TITIVATING, ITALIAN-INSPIRED FORMULA OF MADAGASCAN VANILLA BEANS AND HEAVY CREAM CUT THROUGH WITH LEMON ZEST, SPARKLING PROSECCO, AND A WICKED SPLASH OF LIMONCELLO. SO POTENT, IT WILL LEAVE YOU GURGLING IN A CORNER SLOWLY GOING GAGA.

1 Place the ice cream, Limoncello, prosecco, and lemon juice in a bowl and mix with an immersion blender for 10 seconds.

2 Pour into a champagne saucer and garnish with a raspberry "nipple" surrounded by lemon zest.

3 Enjoy with a chilled shot of Limoncello for medicinal purposes.

Inside scoop

A DEVIL-MAY-CARE BLIZZARD OF MADAGASCAN VANILLA AND LIMONCELLO CUT THROUGH WITH LEMON ZEST AND SPARKLING FIZZ TO FORM THE PERFECT COCKTAIL

USES

VANILLA MONOLOGUES ICE CREAM

PAGE 21

1 teaspoon sesame seeds

½ teaspoons ground cinnamon

2 scoops of Taking the Pistacchio ice cream

dash apricot brandy

dash Italian brandy

SERVES: 1 **PREPARATION:** 10 minutes when the ice cream is already prepared

The Omerta

I ALMOST BECAME BROTHER "MATT THE MONK" WHEN I WAS INVITED TO JOIN A MONASTERY IN A SOCIAL EXPERIMENT BACK IN 2004. A SUBSEQUENT KICK IN THE CLOISTERS ON ACCOUNT OF MY BAD HABITS MEANT I NEVER GOT AROUND TO TAKING MY VOW OF SILENCE—MUCH TO THE CHAGRIN OF MY COLLEAGUES. HOWEVER, EVEN I WOULD BE REDUCED TO FLAGELLATING MYSELF IN BARBED WIRE UNDERPANTS ON THE FLOOR IF I WERE TO BREAK OUR SICILIAN-INSPIRED OMERTA—A COCKTAIL TO RENDER THE MOST OUTSPOKEN COLD WARRIOR SILENT. RESPECTFUL CONTEMPLATION IS THE ORDER OF THE DAY, AND WHILE WE REMAIN OUTSPOKEN IN OUR DEMANDS FOR WHIRLED PEACE, THIS IS ONE CODE OF SILENCE THAT DESERVES TO BE OBEYED. AT LEAST UNTIL YOU'VE LICKED YOUR GLASS CLEAN.

1 Put the sesame seeds into a small, dry saucepan and shake over the heat until they start to brown. Add the cinnamon and toast together for a few more seconds. Set aside.

2 Place the ice cream in a martini glass and add the brandies. Serve sprinkled with the chopped pistacchios and an additional shot of apicot brandy for those in need of fortification.

A RICH, NUTTY, SICILIAN-INFLUENCED ICE CREAM LACED WITH TWO BRANDIES TO CREATE A SOPHISTICATED COCKTAIL FOR THE BROTHERHOOD OF MAN

Inside scoop

USES

TAKING THE PISTACCHIO ICE CREAM

PAGE 30

2 scoops of Chocwork Orange ice cream	**SERVES:** 1 **PREPARATION:** 10 minutes when the ice cream is already prepared
zap of ground cinnamon	
1 shot of ice-cold Grand Marnier liqueur	
zest of ½ an orange	

Fire & Vice

FEEL THE SAND IN YOUR SADDLE AND HOOK UP YOUR CAMEL. THIS ICE CREAM WAS INSPIRED BY A LOST WEEKEND IN THE KALEIDO-SCOPIC JAMAA EL FNA MARKETPLACE IN MARRA-KECH, MOROCCO. A PARADOXICAL CHOCOLATE ICE CREAM COCKTAIL, IT HAS A SUBTLE NORTH AFRICAN INFLUENCE. AFTER DOWNING COPIOUS AMOUNTS OF HOME-BREWED FIG BRANDY WITH MY BERBER GUIDE, THIS CONTRADICTORY IDEA FOR ICE CREAM APPEARED LIKE A MIRAGE ...

1 Place the ice cream in a martini glass and dust with cinnamon.

2 Pour the Grand Marnier into a shot glass, set alight, and pour over the ice cream. Serve decorated with orange zest.

3 Freeze the Grand Marnier for at least an hour beforehand, and enjoy a small glass of it with the ice cream.

Inside scoop GET YOUR PRAYER MATS OUT FOR THIS INCENDIARY-LACED ELIXIR CONSISTING OF RICH CHOCOLATE GANACHE-STYLE ICE CREAM, ORANGE FLAVORS, CINNAMON, AND FLAMING GRAND MARNIER

USES ≫

CHOCWORK ORANGE ICE CREAM

PAGE 28

SUNDAES
DESSERTS

IT'S OUR PHILOSOPHY AT THE ICECREAMISTS THAT LAWS ARE THERE TO BE BROKEN, RULES ARE THERE TO BE BENT, AND EXITS ARE THERE TO BE ENTERED. THEREIN LIES THE SECRET TO OUR MODUS OPERANDI. IN OUR TIME, WE'VE DONE QUESTIONABLE THINGS THAT EXPLORED THE OUTER EXTREMITIES OF THE LAW, GOOD TASTE, AND PUBLIC DECENCY WHEN IT COMES TO ICE CREAM. HOWEVER, IN THE COURSE OF OUR RESEARCH, WE ALSO STUMBLED ACROSS A CORNUCOPIA OF NATURAL BORN CHILLERS THAT WILL LOWER THE BODY TEMPERATURE OF ANY SELF-RESPECTING ICECREAMIST. SO SCOOP ON DOWN WITH OUR KALEIDOSCOPIC COLLECTION OF IGLOO-ROCKING, ICE QUAKES, KILLER CREAMS, AND DESSERT STORMS.

THE RECIPES IN THIS CHAPTER SERVE VARIABLE NUMBERS AND TAKE DIFFERING AMOUNTS OF TIME TO MAKE

VANILLA ICE QUAKE

ICED VANILLA MILK SHAKE

• 1¼ cups ice-cold milk • 3 scoops of Vanilla Monologues ice cream
• ½ teaspoon vanilla extract (optional)

SERVES: 2 PREPARATION: 5 minutes when the ice cream is already prepared

1 Put the milk and ice cream into a blender and blend together.

2 Taste the mixture, then add the vanilla extract, if required. Blend until smooth. Serve in 2 tall glasses with straws.

Inside scoop

PUT THE CHILLA IN VANILLA WITH THIS SEDUCTIVE
ICED REFRESHMENT.

USES ≫

VANILLA
MONOLOGUES
ICE CREAM

PAGE 21

CAFFE ESPRESSO ICE QUAKE

ICED COFFEE MILK SHAKE

• 1¼ cups ice-cold milk • 3 scoops of Espresso Yourself ice cream
2 teaspoons instant espresso powder or coffee granules, to taste • 6 coffee beans, to decorate

SERVES: 2 PREPARATION: 5 minutes when the ice cream is already prepared

1 Put the milk and ice cream into a blender, add the espresso powder or coffee granules, and blend until smooth. Taste, and add more powder or granules if you want a stronger shake.

2 Pour into 2 tall glasses, decorate with the coffee beans, and serve with straws.

Inside scoop

A SUPERCHARGED ICED COFFEE WHIPPED INTO
CREAMY BLISS.

USES ≫

ESPRESSO
YOURSELF
ICE CREAM

PAGE 47

BERRY ICE QUAKE
ICED BERRY MILK SHAKE

· 2½ cups seasonal berries · 3 scoops Glastonberry sorbetto · 6 blueberries, to serve

SERVES: 2 **PREPARATION:** 5 minutes when the ice cream is already prepared

1 Place the berries in a blender, add the sorbetto, and blend until smooth.

2 Pour into 2 glasses and serve with the blueberries on the side.

Inside scoop   YOUR DAILY FREEZE OF REFRESHING SEASONAL BERRIES   USES »   GLASTONBERRY SORBETTO   PAGE 83

CARAMEL ICE QUAKE
ICED DULCE DE LECHE MILK SHAKE

· 1¼ cups ice-cold milk · 3 scoops of Carameltdown ice cream · ground cinnamon, to dust

SERVES: 2 **PREPARATION:** 5 minutes when the ice cream is already prepared

1 Put the milk and ice cream into a blender and blend until smooth.

2 Pour into 2 tall glasses and dust the surface with cinnamon. Serve with straws.

Inside scoop   DULCE DE LECHE-FLAVOR ICE CREAM WHIPPED INTO A FRENZY OF CARAMEL FLAVORS   USES »   CARAMELTDOWN ICE CREAM   PAGE 33

STRAWBERRY ICE QUAKE
ICED STRAWBERRY MILK SHAKE

· 1½ cups hulled strawberries · 1¼ cups ice-cold milk
· 2 scoops of Scarlett Fever ice cream

SERVES: 2 **PREPARATION:** 5 minutes when the ice cream is already prepared

1 Put the strawberries into a blender. Add the milk and ice cream, then blend until smooth.

2 Pour into 2 tall glasses and decorate with a sliced strawberry.

   THE PERFECT MATCH FOR THOSE WITH A SUMMERY DISPOSITION: SUPERCOOL STRAWBERRIES AND CREAM   USES »   SCARLETT FEVER ICE CREAM   PAGE 40

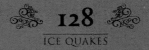

THE JUGGERNAUT
FROZEN HOT CHOCOLATE

OUR CHOCOLATE MELTING POT OF PIPING HOT ENJOYMENT FOR THOSE WHO LIKE TO OVERINDULGE AT A FURIOUS LICK. WE TYPICALLY DELIVER THIS ONE "JUGGERNAUT" STYLE—IN GERMAN BEER GLASSES TOPPED WITH WHIPPED CREAM AND SERVED WITH A COUPLE OF STRAWS. BY THE END OF ONE OF THESE, YOU'LL BE REACHING FOR YOUR STOMACH STAPLER BEFORE LIGHTING A DISTRESS FLARE IN THE DIRECTION OF YOUR NEAREST WEIGHT WATCHERS GROUP.

· 1 cup milk · 6 ounces milk chocolate, finely chopped, plus extra for curls · ½ teaspoon ground cinnamon or ginger (optional) · 1 teaspoon cornstarch · 1 scoop of Sex, Drugs and Choc 'n' Roll ice cream · 1 tablespoon whipped heavy cream

SERVES: 2 PREPARATION: 10 minutes when the ice cream is already prepared

1 Warm half the milk in a saucepan over low heat. Add the chopped chocolate and stir until melted.

2 Whisk in the remaining milk plus the cinnamon or ginger (if using) and cornstarch, and heat until the mixture is warmed through. Use an immersion blender to mix until smooth.

3 Pour into beer glasses or mugs and top with the ice cream. Add a dollop of whipped cream and some chocolate curls. To make chocolate curls, use a vegetable peeler or cheese slicer. For extra punch, lace each of the finished quakes with a shot of Irish cream and serve.

LET HELL FREEZE OVER WITH THIS NO-HOLDS-BARRED ELIXIR OF HOT AND COLD CHOCOLATE FLAVORS THAT WILL STALK YOU RIGHT UP UNTIL YOU COLLAPSE INTO A DIABETIC COMA

USES

SEX, DRUGS AND CHOC 'N' ROLL ICE CREAM

PAGE 26

THE ABOMINABULL SNOWMAN

HIGH ENERGY DRINK

DEFROST YOUR INNER YETI WITH OUR INFAMOUS SEX BOMB ICE CREAM LACED WITH NATURAL STIMULANTS (GINKGO BILOBA, ARGININE, AND GUARANA) AND A CITRUS INFUSION. FUEL INJECTED WITH RED BULL AND BITTERS, THIS MONSTEROUS MIXTURE COULD RAISE GODZILLA FROM HIS GRAVE. THE ULTIMATE IN RECREATIONAL MEDICATION FOR THOSE WITH NARCOLEPTIC TENDENCIES. GRRRR ...

• 2 scoops of Sex Bomb ice cream • ½ cup Red Bull energy drink

• 4 dashes of Spanish or Angostura bitters

• 2 twists of grapefruit, plus finely grated zest (optional)

SERVES: 2   PREPARATION: 5 minutes when the ice cream is already prepared

1 Place the ice cream in a blender. Add the Red Bull and bitters and blend for 10 seconds or until smooth.

2 Pour into a martini glass and serve with a grapefruit twist. Sprinkle with a little grapefruit zest, if you desire.

LEMONY SYLLABUB FLAVOR GIVES WAY TO A CURIOUSLY INVIGORATING COCKTAIL OF RED BULL WITH BITTER NOTES. AN ABOMINABULLY GREAT SUBZERO INTERPRETATION OF AN ENERGY DRINK.

Inside scoop

USES ≫

SEX BOMB
ICE CREAM

PAGE 75

RASPBERRY NIPPLE

VANILLA ICE CREAM SUNDAE

HERE'S THE TITIVATING NONALCOHOLIC "FORMULA MIX" OF OUR INFAMOUS BABY GOOGOO COCKTAIL FUSED WITH BOVINE JUICE, CREAM, MADAGASCAN VANILLA BEANS, ALMONDS, AND JASMINE, THEN CUT WITH LEMON ZEST AND SPICES. SERVED IN A CHAMPAGNE SAUCER WITH A NUTMEG GARNISH AND TOPPED WITH A WICKED RASPBERRY NIPPLE.

- 1 scoop of Vanilla Monologues ice cream
- ½ cup club soda · 2 teaspoons lemon juice
- 1 teaspoon Monin orgeat (almond) syrup · 1 teaspoon Monin jasmine syrup
- 2 dashes of Angostura bitters · 2 teaspoons ground nutmeg, to dust
- 1 fresh raspberry · 1 teaspoon finely grated lemon zest

SERVES: 2 PREPARATION: 5 minutes when the ice cream is already prepared

1 Place the ice cream in a blender. Add the club soda, lemon juice, syrups, and bitters and blend until absolutely smooth.

2 Pour into a champagne saucer and dust the center with nutmeg, using a stencil with a 2-inch hole.

3 Top with a raspberry "nipple" delicately placed in the middle and finish with a pinch of lemon zest.

Inside scoop A HEAVENLY INFUSION OF MADAGASCAN VANILLA, ALMONDS, AND JASMINE, VIOLATED WITH A SOPHISTICATED SHOT OF ANGOSTURA BITTERS TO BALANCE OUT THE SWEETNESS IN THIS FRAGRANT ICED DRINK

USES >> VANILLA MONOLOGUES ICE CREAM

PAGE 31

BABY AFFOGATO

VANILLA ICE CREAM AND COFFEE SUNDAE

AFFOGATO MEANS "DROWNED," AND WHAT BETTER WAY TO
SUBMERGE YOUR SORROWS THAN WITH THIS CLASSIC ITALIAN BLEND
OF ICE CREAM AND FRESH ESPRESSO TOPPED WITH COFFEE BEANS?
A DEPLORABLY INDULGENT WAY TO IMBIBE STIMULANTS.

· 1 small scoop of Vanilla Monologues ice cream · 1 shot of espresso or strong coffee
· 3 coffee beans, to decorate

SERVES: 2   **PREPARATION:** 5 minutes when the ice cream is already prepared

1   Place the ice cream in an espresso cup and pour a shot of freshly made
espresso over the top.

2   Decorate with the coffee beans and serve immediately.

A CLASSIC ITALIAN CONCOCTION OF ANGELIC VANILLA SATURATED WITH ROASTED

COFFEE AROMAS. FOR A STRONGER VERSION USE ESPRESSO YOURSELF

ICE CREAM (SEE PAGE 47).

Inside scoop

USES ≫ VANILLA
MONOLOGUES
ICE CREAM

PAGE 21

THE KNICKERBOCKERGLORYHOLE

KNICKERBOCKER GLORY SUNDAE

DITCH YOUR SOCIAL STRAITJACKET—THIS IS CHOCS IN FROCKS ON THE BLOCK! OUR RETRO-COOL CABARET OF CROSS-DRESSING FLAVORS IS A LASCIVIOUS MIX OF DEVIANT DARK AND WHITE CHOCOLATE ICE CREAMS SANDWICHED TOGETHER IN SEDUCTIVE LAYERS. IT'S PROMISCUOUSLY SERVED STRAIGHT UP, KNICKERBOCKERGLORYHOLE-STYLE, WITH GENEROUS PORTIONS OF HOT CHOCOLATE SAUCE, WHIPPED CREAM, AND OTHER NUT-CRACKING PECCADILLOES, TOPPED WITH A STEMMED MARASCHINO CHERRY UNDER A DRIZZLE OF WHITE CRÈME DE CACAO LIQUEUR. SO IMMORAL AND SEXED UP, IT SHOULD BE BANNED UNDER THE OBSCENITY LAWS, LIKE ALL TOP-SHELF THAWNOGRAPHY.

- 4 ounces milk chocolate, finely chopped · ¼ cup coarsely chopped hazelnuts
- 1 scoop of Choc and Awe ice cream
- 1 scoop of Sex, Drugs and Choc 'n' Roll ice cream · whipped heavy cream
- 1 scoop of Priscilla Cream of the Dessert ice cream · chocolate curls (see page 128)
- 1 stem maraschino cherry · slug of white crème de cacao liqueur

SERVES: 2 PREPARATION: 5 minutes when the ice cream is already prepared

1 Make a sauce by melting the chocolate in a double boiler or a heatproof bowl set over a saucepan of gently simmering water, whisking all the time. Pour half of the sauce into the bottom of a knickerbocker glory glass.

2 Now build layers in the following order: chopped hazelnuts, Choc and Awe ice cream, more chocolate sauce, Sex, Drugs and Choc 'n' Roll ice cream, whipped cream, Priscilla Cream of the Dessert ice cream, more whipped cream, chocolate curls.

3 Top the sundae with the maraschino cherry and finish off with a wicked drizzle of white crème de cacao liqueur.

A NIHILISTIC ORGY OF TRIPLE CHOCOLATE DESTRUCTION BLUDGEONED TOGETHER IN A KNICKERBOCKER GLORY GLASS FOR YOUR DELECTATION

Inside scoop

USES ≫

PRISCILLA QUEEN OF THE DESSERT, CHOC AND AWE, AND SEX, DRUGS, AND CHOC 'N' ROLL ICE CREAMS

PAGES 22, 23, 26

NUCLEAR WINTER
WHITE CHOCOLATE ICE CREAM SUNDAE

A THERMONUCLEAR ICE CREAM CONFLICT BETWEEN THE FORCES OF HOT AND COLD ARMED WITH A CLIMATE-CHANGING ARSENAL OF MOUTHWATERING WEAPONRY. A DESSERT THAT WILL THRILL AND CHILL IN EQUAL MEASURE BEFORE LAUNCHING AN ARSENAL OF CREAMY FRUIT FLAVORS THAT LITERALLY MELT IN YOUR MOUTH. WE CALL THIS ICE CREAM "ARMAGEDDON ON A PLATE." NOW WHERE DID I PUT THOSE LAUNCH CODES ...?

- 1½ cups mixed seasonal berries (raspberries, blackberries, blueberries, etc.)
- 2 ounces white chocolate, finely chopped, plus extra for curls (see page 128)
- 1 tablespoon heavy cream · 1 small scoop of Priscilla Cream of the Dessert ice cream

SERVES: 2 **PREPARATION:** 1 hour for freezing berries, plus 5 minutes when the ice cream is already prepared

1 Spread the berries onto a tray and place in the freezer (on it's coldest setting) for 1 hour, until icy but not completely frozen.

2 When the berries are ready, melt the chocolate in a double boiler or a heatproof bowl set over a saucepan of gently simmering water, whisking all the time. Add the cream and whisk again until blended.

3 Place the frozen berries in 2 glasses or bowls and drizzle the hot chocolate sauce over them. Top with the ice cream and white chocolate curls.

A JUDGMENT DAY BLEND OF MELTING FROZEN BERRIES JUXTAPOSED WITH PIPING HOT WHITE CHOCOLATE SAUCE AND CRISP, COLD WHITE CHOCOLATE ICE CREAM

Inside scoop

USES ≫

PRISCILLA CREAM OF THE DESSERT ICE CREAM

PAGE 22

MANTECATO ITALIANO

ITALIAN CREMA ICE CREAM SUNDAE

I HAVE ALWAYS FOUND SOLACE IN THE WORDS OF SKY MASTERSON, MARLON BRANDO'S CHARACTER IN THE MOVIE "GUYS AND DOLLS," WHO SAID, "AS MY DADDY USED TO SAY, THE ONLY TIME YOU NEED TO BE IN A HURRY IS WHEN THE POLICE ARE COMING UP THE STAIRS." WHEN I WAS ON THE RUN FROM THE POLICE IN ITALY, EMERGENCY COLD RELIEF APPEARED IN THE FORM OF OUR GELATO MASTER, THE INIMITABLE ROBERTO LOBRANO, WHO WHISKED ME FROM MY HOTEL TO A SMALL RESTAURANT ON THE EDGE OF BOLOGNA AND INTRODUCED ME TO THIS ITALIAN EPIC THAT MOVED AT A GLACIAL SPEED, BEFORE BEING BEATEN INTO SUBMISSION BEFORE MY EYES. THIS ICE CREAM IS SO REVELATORY IN ITS SIMPLICITY THAT I AM INSISTING ON HAVING IT AS MY FINAL MEAL BEFORE THEY PLUG MY CHAIR IN.

- **4 large scoops of The Custardy Suite ice cream**
- **2 tablespoons good-quality balsamic vinegar**

SERVES: 2   PREPARATION: 5 minutes when the ice cream is already prepared

1 Place the ice cream in a large bowl, add the vinegar, and fold together using a spoon or wire whisk. As the ice cream softens, whisk until the mixture becomes soft and slightly fluffy, like whipped cream. This will take a few minutes.

2 Taste the mixture, adding more vinegar to taste, if you desire, then pour gently in folds into 2 glasses. Consume to anything from Puccini's La Boheme …

THE GREATEST VERSE OF ITALIAN POETRY EVER WRITTEN. RICH, THICK, EGGY ICE CREAM THAT

SOARS TO VERTIGINOUS NEW HEIGHTS WITH THE HELP OF AN UNEXPECTED

AND UPLIFTING CHORUS OF BALSAMIC VINEGAR.

Inside scoop

USES »

THE CUSTARDY SUITE ICE CREAM

PAGE 36

THE FEDERICI

CHOCOLATE AND AMARETTO ICE CREAM SUNDAE

ICE CREAM EVANGELIST ANTONIO FEDERICI FIRST GOT RELIGION WHEN HE CREATED HIS OWN GELATO IN 1896 IN THE MOUNTAINS CLOSE TO THE ITALIAN RIVIERA AND THE HIP RESORTS OF PORTOFINO AND RAPALLO. SINCE THAT EPIPHANY, FAITHFUL DISCIPLES HAVE DEDICATED THEIR LIVES TO SPREADING HIS "GOSPEL OF COOL" AS THEY HAND OUT SPOONFULS OF FRESHLY MADE ARTISAN GELATO TO THE INFIDELS AND UNCONVERTED. IT HAS SUBSEQUENTLY BECOME THE RELIGION OF CHOICE FOR RECOVERING CATHOLICS AND LAPSED ALCOHOLICS. TO MARK THIS GLOBAL COMMUNION, WE CREATED OUR OWN HOMAGE TO THE MAN HIMSELF WITH A SUNDAE SERVICE YOU CAN TRULY BELIEVE IN. AMEN.

- 10 amaretti cookies · Amaretto liqueur
- 2 large scoops of Priscilla Cream of the Dessert ice cream · 1 sheet edible gold leaf

FOR THE COMMUNION WAFER AND WINE
- 1 ounce white chocolate · ¼ cup Frangelico (hazelnut liqueur)
- 2 tablespoons Amaretto liqueur · 1 large scoop of Priscilla Cream of the Dessert ice cream

SERVES: 2 PREPARATION: 10 minutes when the ice cream is already prepared

1 First make the "communion wafer." Melt the chocolate in a double boiler or a heatproof bowl set over a saucepan of gently simmering water, whisking all the time. Using a spatula, spread the chocolate thinly over a sheet of parchment paper and put in the refrigerator to harden (about 60 minutes). When set, dip a 1¼–2-inch-diameter round cutter in hot water and cut out 2 chocolate disks. Set aside.

2 Meanwhile, make the "communion wine" by putting the Frangelico, Amaretto, and Priscilla Cream of the Dessert ice cream into a blender and pulsing until the mixture is smooth and creamy. Taste with a teaspoon and adjust as necessary, adding more alcoho,l if required. Keep in the refrigerator while doing steps 3 and 4.

3 Put the amaretti cookies into a bowl and drizzle with the Amaretto liqueur. Set aside.

4 Place both ice creams in another bowl, let stand at room temperature for 5 minutes, then gently fold one into the other and mix in the gold leaf.

5 Place the mixture in 2 chalices or glasses and crumble in the moistened cookies. Top with the chocolate communion wafer and serve with a slug of communion wine alongside.

PRISCILLA CREAM
OF THE DESSERT
AND CHOC AND
AWE. ICE CREAM
PAGES 22, 23

A REVELATORY BLEND OF BITTER-RICH DARK CHOCOLATE, SWEET AMARETTO, AND A
COMMUNION WINE THAT WILL HAVE YOU LINING UP AT THE ALTAR FOR
REFILLS UNTIL JUDGMENT DAY

Inside scoop

USES ≫

ROCK 'N' ROYAL
VANILLA ICE CREAM SANDWICH

ATTENTION, LOYAL SUBJECTS! HAVEN'T GOT AN INVITATION? NOT ON THE GUEST LIST? IT NEVER STOPPED MY LYCRA-PAL ASSOCIATES FROM VISITING THE ROYAL BALCONY AT BUCKINGHAM PALACE FOR AFTERNOON TEA ONE DAY BACK IN 2004. THE ROCK 'N' ROYAL ICE CREAM SANDWICH WAS INSPIRED BY THE CITY'S POLICING POLICY AT THE SCOOPING OF THE COLOR (ONE PROTESTOR SANDWICHED BETWEEN TWO COPPERS).

- 1 large scoop of Vanilla Monologues ice cream
- 2 soft chocolate cookies (the softest you can find)

SERVES: 2   **PREPARATION:** 5 minutes when the ice cream is already prepared

1   Press the ice cream face down on one of the cookies and spread evenly with a knife until it reaches the edge. Press the second cookie on top to form a sandwich. If you can't find really soft cookies, make the sandwich with firm ones and put in the freezer for several hours until frozen. Remove and let soften for 10 minutes before serving.

2   For maximum effect, use a knife to trim the sandwich into a square shape, then slice into 2 triangles and serve on a plate.

Inside scoop   LET THEM EAT KATE, WITH THIS TREASONOUS ICE CREAM SANDWICH FOR THE COMMON PEOPLE THAT IS MOST DEFINITELY NOT BY ROYAL APPOINTMENT. (PLEASE VISIT ME IN THE TOWER WHEN I'M CAUGHT.)

USES ≫

VANILLA
MONOLOGUES
ICE CREAM

PAGE 21

DEEP-FRIED ICE CREAM
VANILLA ICE CREAM BALLS

AS MY EXWIFE ONCE SAID, "SHIT HUSBAND. GREAT COCKTAILS." AN EPITAPH FOR MY GRAVESTONE IF EVER THERE WAS ONE, AND THIS HISTORIC RECIPE WAS ONE OF HER FAVORITES. MORE ADDICTIVE THAN CRACK COCAINE AND HOTTER THAN SATAN'S JOCKSTRAP, THESE INCENDIARY BALLS OF FIRE WILL WARM YOUR FROZEN PARTS AT 50 PACES.

· 4 small scoops of Vanilla Monologues ice cream · 28 graham crackers (7 ounces)
· 2 eggs · 1 tablespoon whole milk · sunflower oil, for deep-frying
· confectioners' sugar, to dust · ¼ cup Dulce de Leche sauce, warmed (see page 154)

SERVES: 2   PREPARATION: 5 minutes when the ice cream is already prepared

1 Line a tray that will fit in your freezer with parchment paper. Quickly roll the ice cream scoops into balls, place on the tray, and put in the freezer for 2–4 hours, or until frozen to the touch.

2 Meanwhile, crush the cookies in a bowl until you have fine crumbs.

3 Remove the ice cream balls from the freezer and quickly roll them in the crumbs, making sure each one is properly coated before freezing again for 1 hour.

4 When the balls are frozen, whisk the eggs and milk together in a bowl. Coat each ball in the egg mixture, shake off any excess, then roll in the crumbs again. Return to the freezer for another hour.

5 Fill a large saucepan halfway with sunflower oil and heat until it reaches 390°F, or a cube of bread dropped into the oil browns in about 30 seconds. When ready, fry two ice cream balls at a time for around 15 seconds, or until golden. Remove with a slotted spoon and roll on paper towels to remove any excess oil.

6 Serve immediately, drizzled with the Dulce de Leche sauce and dusted with confectioners' sugar. To spice up the sundae, dust with a little cinnamon.

Inside scoop HOT, CRISP COOKIE CRUNCH GIVES WAY TO SOFT, COOLING VANILLA ICE CREAM. THIS IS TOP-SHELF THAWNOGRAPHY AT ITS MOST OBSCENE. FIRE-RETARDANT CLOTHING OPTIONAL.

USES >> VANILLA MONOLOGUES ICE CREAM

PAGE 21

THE SCOOPERBOWL

CHOCOLATE FONDUE WITH ICE CREAM

SAVE THE WORLD FROM MELTDOWN WITH OUR DOUBLE-DIPPING CAULDRON OF SAUCY SEDUCTION THAT VIOLATES EVERY RULE IN YOUR AVERAGE ICE CREAM MAN'S INSTRUCTION MANUAL.

· **12 scoops ice cream of your choice** · **$\frac{1}{3}$ cup heavy cream**
· **12 ounces dark or milk chocolate, finely chopped** · **selection of fresh fruit, cut into chunks**

SERVES: 2–4 **PREPARATION:** 2–4 hours for the ice cream balls; 20 minutes for the sauce

I Line a tray that will fit in your freezer with parchment paper. Quickly roll the ice cream scoops into balls, place on the tray, and put in the freezer for 2–4 hours, or until frozen to the touch.

2 When the balls are frozen, warm the cream in a saucepan over low heat until hot but not boiling. Add the chocolate and whisk until melted. Transfer the sauce to a fondue pot that is heated by a low flame.

3 Arrange the fresh fruit and the ice cream balls on separate plates around the pot. Using a fondue fork, quickly dip the ice cream, then the fruit into the warm sauce and devour immediately.

IT'S ENOUGH TO SEND YOU STIR CRAZY—WAVE AFTER WAVE OF MORALLY HAZARDOUS COCOA FLAVORS RECLINING IN A SEXUALLY AMBIGUOUS SOCIAL SETTING. NOW WHO'S GOT MY CAR KEYS AND WHERE'S MY WIFE?

Inside scoop

POPS

I WAS ON A MISSION TO SWEDEN WHEN I INEXPLICABLY FOUND MYSELF ON A SMALL PLANE HEADING TOWARD THE ARCTIC CIRCLE AND THE WORLD FAMOUS ICE HOTEL. ON ARRIVAL, I ATTRACTED CURIOUS STARES FROM OTHER GUESTS ON ACCOUNT OF THE FACT THAT THEY WERE DRESSED TO CHILL IN SKI WEAR, AND I WAS DRESSED TO THRILL IN A BLACK LEATHER TRENCH COAT AND T-SHIRT. GIVEN IT WAS MINUS 40 DEGREES OUTSIDE AND ONLY 25 DEGREES INSIDE, THE ESKIMO AT THE ICE BAR TOLD ME VODKA DIDN'T FREEZE AND WOULD PRESERVE ME SAFELY FOR THE NIGHT AND PRESCRIBED ME ENOUGH ABSOLUT VODKA TO PARALYZE A BABY MAMMOTH. THE TRIP TO SWEDEN NEARLY COST ME MY LIFE, BUT MY LOVE OF ALL THINGS SUBZERO HAD BEEN FROZEN IN MY IMAGINATION THESE ARE SOME OF OUR HOTTEST LICKS FOR DISCERNING COLD WARRIORS. ENJOY!

YOU CAN ALSO USE OUR SORBETTO MIXES TO FREEZE MORE OF YOUR ASSETS, IF YOU DESIRE.

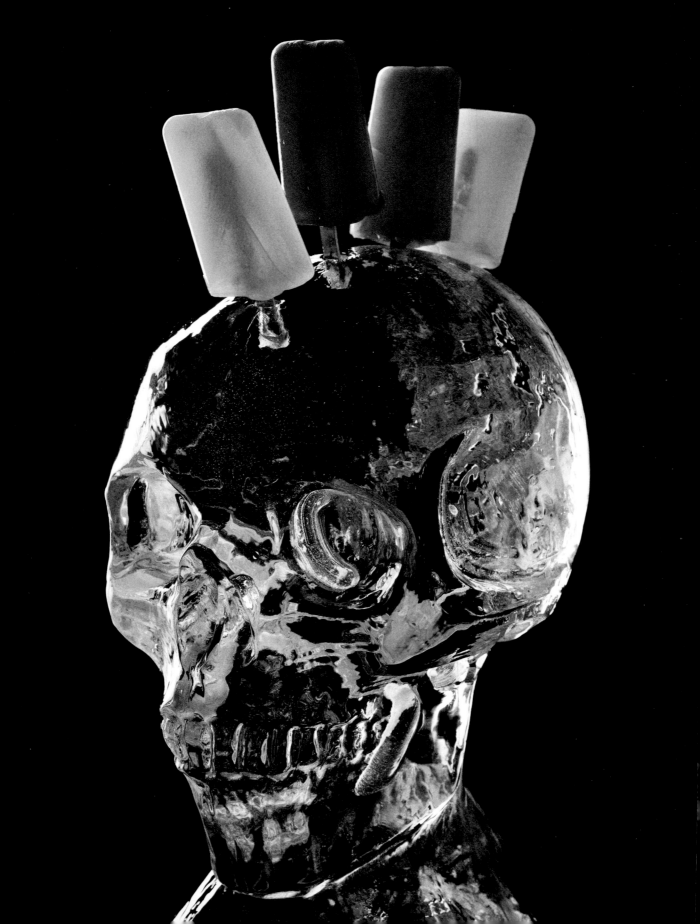

JOHN LEMON
LEMONADE ICE POPS

• 1¼ cups water • 1¼ cups superfine or granulated sugar
• 1 cup freshly squeezed lemon juice
• dash of concentrated lime juice, to taste

MAKES: 6-8 PREPARATION: 10 minutes,
plus about 1 hour freezing

1 Pour the water into a saucepan and add the sugar.
Place over low heat and bring to a boil, whisking
often, until the sugar dissolves. Reduce the heat and
let simmer for 5 minutes, continuing to whisk until
the liquid turns into a syrup. Set aside and let cool
for 10 minutes.

2 Add the lemon juice and lime juice to the sugar
syrup and whisk together. Pour into ice pop molds,
filling them about two-thirds full so that the mixture
has room to expand as it freezes. Place in the freezer
for about 30 minutes, until almost solid, then insert
a stick in each one. Freeze for another 30 minutes.

BABY BRAIN FREEZE
WATERMELON ICE POPS

• ½ cup water • ½ cup superfine or granulated sugar
• flesh from 1 watermelon, seeds discarded
• juice of 1 lime

MAKES: 6-8 PREPARATION: 10 minutes,
plus about 1 hour freezing

1 Follow step 1 (above). Put the watermelon flesh
in a blender, pulse until crushed, then strain into a
measuring cup. You should have about 2 cups of juice.

2 Add the watermelon and lime juices to the sugar
syrup and whisk together. Pour into ice pop molds,
filling them about two-thirds full so that the mixture
has room to expand as it freezes. Place in the freezer
for about 30 minutes, until almost solid, then insert
a stick in each one. Freeze for another 30 minutes.

AGENT ORANGE
ORANGE ICE POPS

• 1 cup water • 1¼ cups superfine or granulated sugar
• 1 cup freshly squeezed orange juice
• dash of ginger syrup, to taste (optional)

MAKES: 6-8 PREPARATION: 10 minutes,
plus about 1 hour freezing

1 Follow step 1 (left).

2 Add the orange juice and ginger syrup to the sugar
syrup and whisk together. Pour into ice pop molds,
filling them about two-thirds full so that the mixture
has room to expand as it freezes. Place in the freezer
for about 30 minutes, until almost solid, then insert a
stick in each one. Freeze for another 30 minutes.

THE PHANTOM RASPBERRY BLOWER
RASPBERRY ICE POPS

• 1 cup water • 1¼ cups superfine or granulated sugar
• 8 cups raspberries (about 3 pints)
• juice of 1 lemon
• dash of elderflower syrup, to taste (optional)

MAKES: 6-8 PREPARATION: 10 minutes,
plus about 1 hour freezing

1 Follow step 1 (above left). Place the raspberries
in a blender and pulse until crushed, then strain
into a measuring cup. You should have about 2 cups
of juice.

2 Add the raspberry juice, lemon juice, and
elderflower syrup (if using) to the sugar syrup and
whisk together. Pour into ice pop molds, filling them
about two-thirds full so that the mixture has room
to expand as it freezes. Place in the freezer for about
30 minutes, until almost solid, then insert a stick in
each one. Freeze for another 30 minutes.

FIZZ MUST BE LOVE
PINK CHAMPAGNE ICE POPS

THE RESTAURANT RECEIPT READ, "6 BOTTLES LAURENT PERRIER CUVÉE ROSE BRUT NV CHAMPAGNE, 16 DOUBLE COGNACS. THANK YOU FOR YOUR CUSTOM, WE HOPE YOU ENJOYED YOUR MEAL." BACK IN THE HALCYON DAYS OF THE 1990S, LIQUID LUNCHING WASN'T JUST A PASTIME, IT WAS A SPORT FOR THOSE WITH AN APPETITE FOR DESTRUCTION. THANKFULLY, I DON'T DRINK ANYMORE, BUT I DON'T DRINK ANY LESS EITHER. IF WE COULD HAVE STUCK A BOTTLE OF CHAMPAGNE ON AN ICE POP STICK, WE WOULD HAVE, INSTEAD, WE HAD TO COMPROMISE WITH A GLASS OF THE PINK STUFF ON A STICK.

· ½ cup water · ⅓ cup superfine or granulated sugar
· 1¾ cupd pink Champagne (Laurent-Perrier rosé or similar)

MAKES: 6-8 **PREPARATION:** 10 minutes, plus about 1 hour freezing

1 Pour the water into a saucepan and add the sugar. Place over low heat and bring to a boil, whisking often, until the sugar dissolves. Reduce the heat and let simmer for 5 minutes, continuing to whisk until the liquid turns into a syrup. Set aside and let cool for 10 minutes.

2 Add the champagne and whisk together. Pour into ice pop molds, filling them about two-thirds full so that the mixture has room to expand as it freezes. Place in the freezer for about 30 minutes, until almost solid, then insert a stick in each one. Freeze for another 30 minutes.

If you can't find pink Champagne, use ordinary Champagne and add a splash of crème de cassis.

I DON'T DRINK WATER. HAVE YOU SEEN THE WAY IT RUSTS PIPES? W. C. FIELDS

A DECADENT KICK OF CHAMPAGNE WITH A SOFT HINT OF FIZZ AND GRAPE AND A SUGARY FINISH

Inside scoop

SHOOT TO CHILL
ABSINTHE ICE POPS

THEY SAY ABSINTHE MAKES THE HEART GROW FONDER. AFTER A COUPLE OF THESE YOU MIGHT GO ABSINTHE WITHOUT LEAVE IN THE NEAREST ASYLUM WITH YOUR FELT TIPS LIKE VAN GOGH, WHO WAS SAID TO PAINT UNDER A BURNING GREEN ABSINTHE HAZE. FEAR NOT, WHATEVER CRIME OR MISDEMEANOR YOU HAVE COMMITTED, WE ONLY SHOOT TO CHILL WITH OUR SACRED GUN VICE POPS. WE'VE TONED THE ABSINTHE QUOTA DOWN FOR A BETTER-BALANCED ICE POP.

• 2 ½ cups water • ½ cup superfine or granulated sugar
• ½ cup Midori (melon liqueur) • ¼ cup absinthe, or to taste

MAKES: 6-8 **PREPARATION:** 10 minutes, plus about 1 hour freezing

I Pour ½ cup of the water into a saucepan and add the sugar. Place over low heat and bring to a boil, whisking often, until the sugar dissolves. Reduce the heat and let simmer for 5 minutes, continuing to whisk until the liquid turns into a syrup. Set aside and let cool for 10 minutes.

2 Add the remaining water, the Midori, and absinthe to the syrup and whisk together. Pour into ice pop molds, filling them about two-thirds full so that the mixture has room to expand as it freezes. Place in the freezer for about 30 minutes, until almost solid, then insert a stick in each one. Freeze for another 30 minutes.

For a more potent effect, reduce the amount of water you add to the syrup.

BECOME A POP STAR

Inside scoop FOR THOSE LESS ROMANTICALLY INCLINED, IT WILL ALSO DELAY THE ONSET OF RIGOR MORTIS, PROVIDING AN ADRENALINE SHOT OF THE MIRACULOUS AND THE MEDICINAL WITH ANISE AND WORMWOOD FLAVORS FINISHED WITH A SWEET, LOVING LICK OF MELON

SOMETHING SAUCY

CHOC 'N' ROLL SAUCE
DARK CHOCOLATE SAUCE

THIS MELTING POT OF CHOC 'N' ROLL SAUCE IS POSSESSED BY A SUPERNATURAL POWER THAT COULD HEAL THE SICK, RAISE THE DEAD, AND LEAVE TONGUES FIRMLY EMBEDDED IN THE CHEEKS OF THE BEAUTIFUL AND THE DAMNED.

- 8 ounces dark or milk chocolate, finely chopped
- ¾ cup whole milk • 2 tablespoons heavy cream
- 2½ tablespoons superfine or granulated sugar
- 2½ tablespoons butter, chopped into small pieces

MAKES: 1 cup PREPARATION: 5 minutes

1 Melt the chocolate in a double boiler or heatproof bowl set over a saucepan of gently simmering water, whisking all the time. Remove from the heat and whisk in the milk, cream, and sugar. Return to the heat and stir gently for a few seconds. Remove from the heat again and stir in the butter, a few pieces at a time, until you have a smooth sauce.

2 Strain and serve immediately with ice cream, or keep warm in a bain-marie until needed. Fuel inject the sauce, if you desire, with a slug of Grand Marnier, Amaretto, or Baileys Irish Cream.

HOLD YOUR BREATH FOR THIS FRENZIED BLAST OF COCOA FLAVORS DISTILLED INTO A CHOCOLATE SAUCE THAT MAKES *Inside scoop* FOR THE PERFECT HOT TUB FOR ANY OF OUR ICE CREAMS.

DULCHE DE LECHE SAUCE
CARAMEL SAUCE

HOW NOW BROWN COW? CARAMELIZE YOUR SOUL WITH THIS INTOXICATING SWEET MILK SAUCE FOR INCURABLE LECHE ADDICTS. WHATEVER I OPT FOR IN THE WAY OF STIMULANTS OR NOCTURNAL ACTIVITIES, THIS STICKY SAUCE WILL ALWAYS BE ONE OF MY PRINCIPAL DRUGS OF CHOICE—A TONGUE-TWISTING LICKETY-SPLIT FROM SOUTH OF THE EQUATOR.

- 1 (14-ounce) can sweetened condensed milk
- sea salt • ground cinnamon (optional)

MAKES: about 1¾ cups PREPARATION: 1 hour and 10 minutes

1 Heat the oven to 325°F. Pour the milk into a small, shallow baking dish and add a little sea salt. Place the dish within a larger dish and fill with enough boiled hot water to reach about halfway up the sides of the small dish. Cover with aluminum foil and bake for 1 hour, until browned, checking occasionally and adding more water to the large dish, if required.

2 Remove from the oven and let the small dish cool for 5 minutes before whisking the contents until smooth. Dust lightly with cinnamon (if using), then serve with ice cream. The sauce will keep for up to 3 days in the refrigerator. To warm, put in a heatproof bowl and flash in a microwave for a few seconds on High, or warm in a bain-marie.

SWEET, SIMMERING CARAMEL NOTES PULSATING IN A DELIRIOUSLY STEAMY SAUCE TO *Inside scoop* A SAMBA BEAT

INGREDIENTS & BASIC TOOLS

All of the ingredients in the book come from well-known food retailers, delis, or online stores.

Alcohol: The intoxicant of choice for any self-respecting icecreamist, alcohol is a superior carrier of many flavors. It will depress the freezing point of any ice cream or sorbet, resulting in a softer scoop. It has to be used sparingly—overindulge and the ice cream won't freeze; get it right and you will be transported to new heights of advanced refreshment.

Cream: Always use the best heavy cream available.

Eggs: Use free-range where possible; the yolks add richness and structure to ice cream. The whites are not used, so save them to make meringues. Separating eggs is easy. Set out two bowls. Crack the center of an egg gently on the rim of a bowl and use your thumbs to gently pry the shell apart. Move the yolk back and forth between the shell halves, letting the white drip into the bowl below. Place the yolk in the other bowl.

Milk: Use whole milk—nothing less is acceptable.

Sugar: Critically, it allows for ice cream to be scooped at subzero temperatures without it turning into ice. In a sorbetto, sugar unleashes a blitzkrieg of riotous fruit flavors to the front of the palate. In general, use superfine sugar because it dissolves quickly, enhances flavor, improves texture, and lowers the freezing point of ice cream. If you only have granulated sugar, process equal quantities in a blender for 60 seconds to make superfine sugar. Occasionally, brown sugar, which is deliciously sticky and dark, replaces superfine sugar in certain recipes.

Vanilla beans: Use the best you can find (ideally Madagascan), which can be found in major food retailers. The beans are slit with a knife and the seeds then scraped into the custard mixture so they can infuse their flavor. If you can't find vanilla beans, you could use vanilla extract, but use it sparingly to flavor to your satisfaction.

Bowls: Preferably large and one of that is heatproof; plastic bowls are fine for separating and beating the eggs and making and chilling the custard in your refrigerator.

Cheesecloth: For straining very fine custard mixtures (usually recipes with nuts in).

Chef's knife: 8–10 inches, for scraping vanilla beans, preparing fruit, and chopping other ingredients.

Food thermometer: Preferably digital, to dip into the mixture (not touching the pan) when cooking the base mix.

Refrigerator/freezer thermometer: For checking that your refrigerator and freezer are set at the correct temperature. The refrigerator should be 40°F and your freezer 0°F.

Grater: For preparing citrus zest.

Heavy saucepan: For making the base mix.

Immersion blender: Electric and handheld—for mixing ingredients into the custard and for pureeing fruit.

Measuring cups and spoons: A set of cups for measuring dry ingredients, a liquid measuring cup for liquids, and spoons for both.

Mixer: Electric for beating the eggs and the base mixture.

Plastic containers: You'll need a lot, at least 1-quart capacity and with lids, for freezing and storing ice cream.

Scoop: While we prefer using an Italian-style spatula, you might find it easier to use a scoop, especially once your ice cream has been frozen. I always keep a couple on hand, ready to dip into warm water for a quicker, smoother scoop when guests are around.

Spatula: Silicone and heatproof, the wider the better, to scrape out and serve the ice cream.

Spoons: A wooden spoon is essential for stirring the base mixture; you can never have enough teaspoons and tablespoons, especially for tasting the custards and the final product.

Strainers: One fine, one medium.

ICE CREAM MACHINES

Countertop Models

In general these are a relatively small investment for a decent little machine (buy the best you can afford). It comes with a canister of refrigerant that must be kept upright.

The canister must be prefrozen for 12–24 hours before churning ingredients. The churning mechanism is also a little flimsy and will struggle with heavy mixes. We recommend buying at least two canisters so that you can make more than one ice cream on the same day. If you can't buy the canisters at the time you buy the machine, they are easily available online.

Once you have chilled your base mixture (see page 14), these machines will churn great ice creams in about 40–60 minutes.

Continuous Models

A continuous compressor-style machine has a built-in refrigeration unit that doesn't need prefreezing. This allows for you to make as many ice creams a day as you like (provided your base mixture has been chilled correctly; see page 14). It also makes the ice cream faster and can deal with thicker ice cream mixes, thus giving you greater flexibility. Some machines let you remove the lid to add ingredients during churning instead of adding them through a small opening.

The disadvantages are that it's a big-ticket item for your kitchen; it's not small and can be noisy; it must be handled carefully, kept upright, and generally allowed to settle for 12 hours after transit. This type of a machine is a serious piece of kitchen equipment for serious icecreamists.

On the plus side, the machine will churn great ice creams in 20–60 minutes, depending on how chilled your base mixture is and provided the chill switch has been switched on at least 5 minutes before use.

I CAN RESIST EVERYTHING EXCEPT TEMPTATION. OSCAR WILDE

TROUBLE-SHOOTING

When making ice cream, it is possible that the process could be affected by a number of different factors. The following are the most common scenarios and the questions that our icereamists sometimes ask themselves.

WHY ISN'T MY ICE CREAM FREEZING?

» Your ingredients are warm. If your ingredients are at room temperature or above, the ambient temperature is too warm, and this can adversely affect your ice cream. Try to make sure all your ingredients are seriously chilled before use.

» Your equipment is warm. Make sure the freezer container has been frozen long enough in the freezer, as well as the plastic container or canister of refrigerant. If it hasn't, then the ice cream won't freeze properly.

» Your ambient temperature is warm. A warm kitchen can also slow down the freezing process in the ice cream machine.

WHY HAS MY ICE CREAM MACHINE STOPPED OR IS STRUGGLING TO CHURN?

» Check your quantities. Adding too much mixture to the machine can slow it down and cause it to stop. If this happens, remove some of the mixture and continue churning.

» Check your mixture. Some mixtures are rich and heavy, so if the machine slows down or stops, remove some of the mixture.

I DON'T KNOW WHAT'S WRONG AND I'VE TRIED ALL THE ABOVE

» In a worst-case scenario, use plan B: pour the mixture in a freezerproof container with a lid, place in the lowest compartment of your freezer (where it is coldest) and turn the freezer to its lowest setting. Check every few hours, stirring to see if the ice cream is smooth and silky. Plan B, regrettably, does not compensate for blackouts.

INDEX

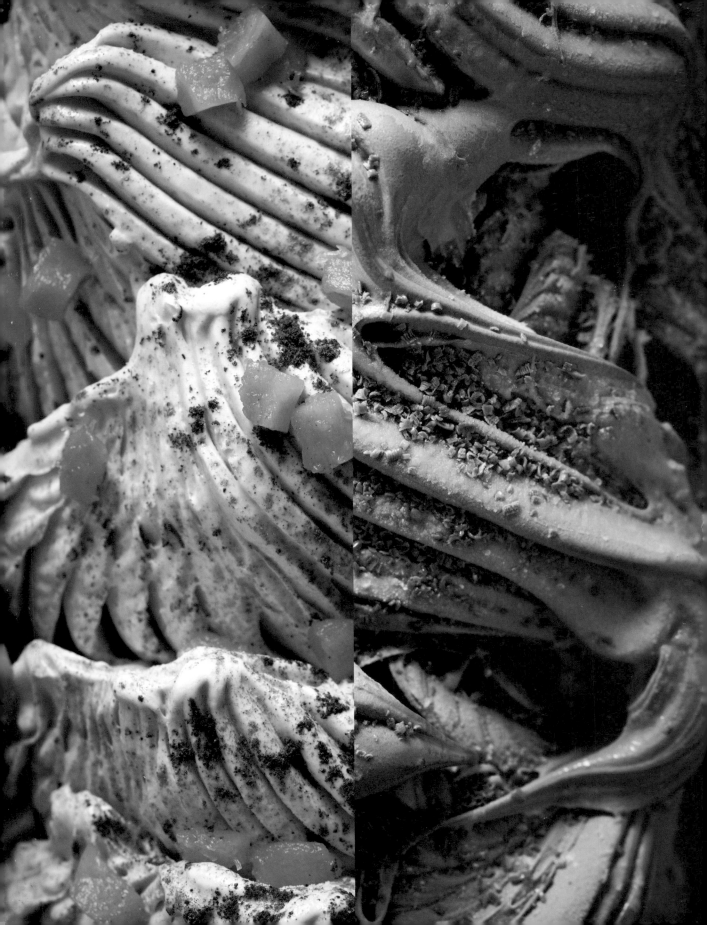